# My Style

I love creating intricate black and white floral designs that start with focal points such as animals, faces, inspirational quotes, or mandalas. I always begin with a subject in mind, then add botanical details in the background. Some of my pieces are inspired by famous buildings around the world, and others are works of fantasy-inspired doodle art featuring forests, parks, waterfalls, etc. And I can't get enough of bold and bright colors on my drawings!

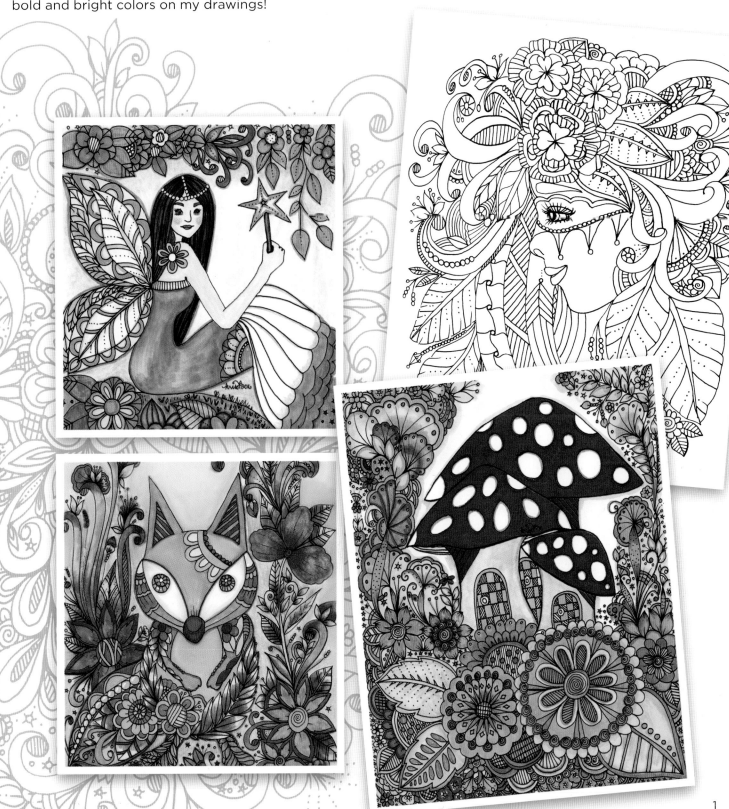

# My Favorite Coloring Supplies

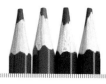

Here's a quick look at some of my preferred coloring media. But don't forget! You can also use crayons, water-based markers, gel pens . . . anything you like!

- **Fine-point felt-tip pens:** Some of us love adding patterns on drawings while coloring; felt-tip pens are great for that. They are also good for adding colors inside small, detailed areas.

- **Colored pencils:** For a smooth coloring experience, I highly recommend colored pencils. They are very easy to blend and great for layering colors.

- **Brush markers:** These are your best choice if you want to achieve bright and vivid colors. Depending on the brand that you use, they are very blendable. My favorites are Winsor & Newton and Copic Sketch markers.

- **Chisel-tip markers:** These are good for coloring large areas. With the various angles of the tip, you can get three types of stroke: broad, medium, and thin. Colorless chisel-tip markers are also great to use as a blending tool.

- **Water-soluble pastels:** If you want to add a splash of watercolor to your designs, use water-soluble pastels. They act like crayons when dry, but you have the option of applying water to add a watercolor wash to your work, and they are very easy to manipulate. You can even use an alcohol-based blender pen or a paper blending stump to blend the colors.

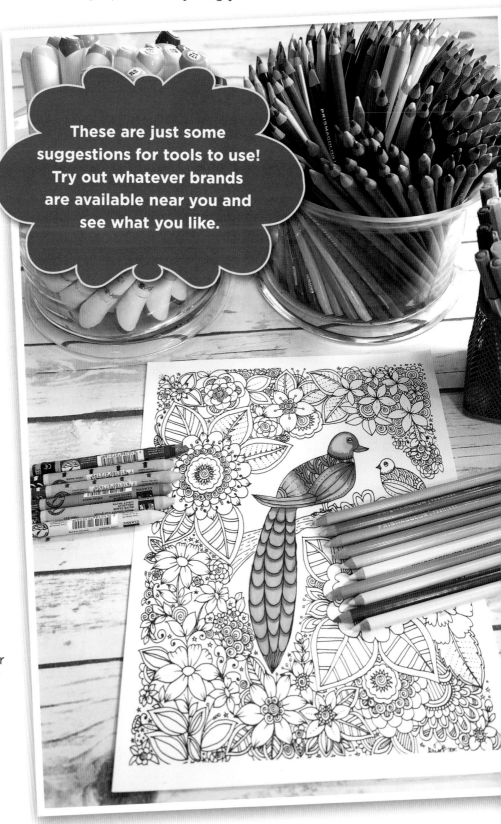

These are just some suggestions for tools to use! Try out whatever brands are available near you and see what you like.

# Coloring Tips

Choose a color palette if you're unsure of what colors to use. There are tons of color palettes online, or let a photo or object inspire you! For this design, I selected a mini-palette for different areas of the design and put them all together to make sure they'd work well.

Don't be afraid to mix and match colors!

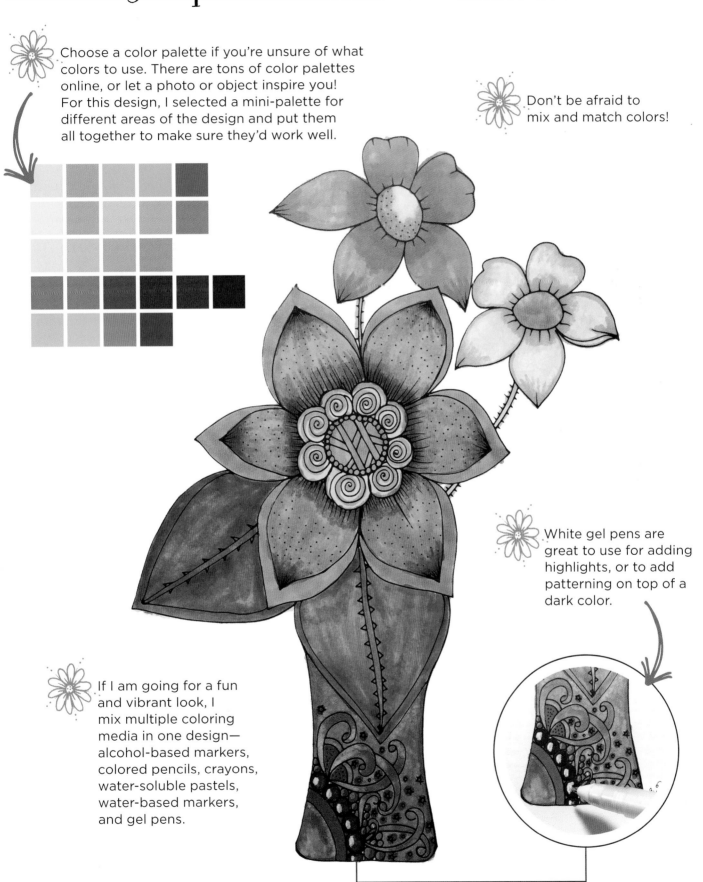

White gel pens are great to use for adding highlights, or to add patterning on top of a dark color.

If I am going for a fun and vibrant look, I mix multiple coloring media in one design—alcohol-based markers, colored pencils, crayons, water-soluble pastels, water-based markers, and gel pens.

# How to Blend

I'm always going for the well-blended look. To achieve this, I use a good blender, though you can also blend without a blender by simply using several different shades of a single color and building up a gradient with them. But I like to use an **alcohol-based blender marker** with almost every coloring medium and design that I do. Blenders with chiseled tips are my favorite because they are versatile— you can get thick and thin lines and blends out of them. I usually begin with light pastel shades no matter what medium I'm using. That way I can slowly build the colors to bright, bold tones.

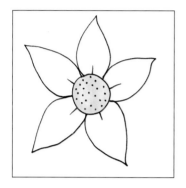

**1.** Fill the center of the flower with a light color, like this yellow.

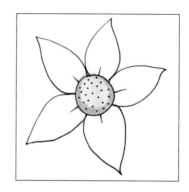

**2.** Now use a darker color to go around the inner edges of the flower center, on top of the light color.

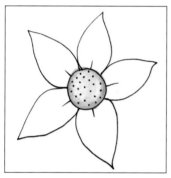

**3.** Blend the colors using a blending tool such as a blending marker, using gentle strokes and moving your tool from dark to light.

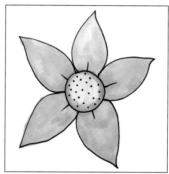

**4.** Fill in the petals with a new light color, like this orange.

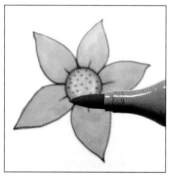

**5.** Now use a darker color, like this dark orange, around the outer edges of the center of the flower.

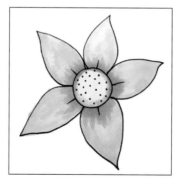

**6.** This darker color at the base of the petals gives the flower dimensional, realistic "shadows."

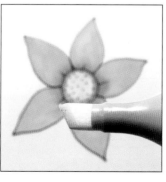

**7.** Blend the colors using a blending tool such as a blending marker— chisel tips like this one are my favorite.

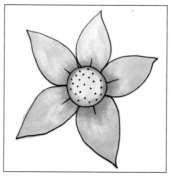

**8.** Your beautifully blended flower is done!

4

# Coloring Skin Tones

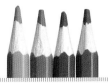

I think it's a good idea to start with light colors when it comes to skin tones. Slowly build up the colors until you get the effect you want on the drawing. It's also a good idea to "swatch" the colors before proceeding. Below is the skin tone palette I used for this drawing.

Base        └─ Shadows ─┘        Blush

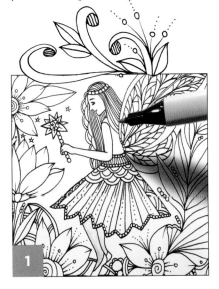

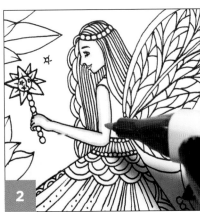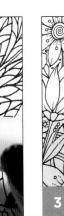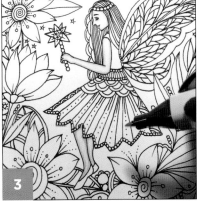

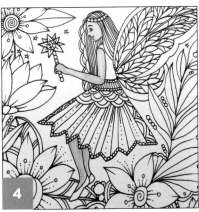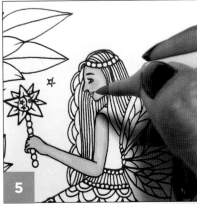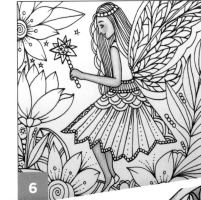

1. Pick a skin tone color that's lighter than your desired final effect as a starting point. Here, I chose a very pale peachy color.

2. Fill the whole surface of the skin with that color, not pressing too hard.

3. Add shadows by outlining the skin edges in a slightly darker shade of the same color.

4. Carefully blend the colors together until you are satisfied with the effect.

5. If you'd like, add blush on the checks with a darker, pinker tone, and blend.

6. You're done with your lifelike skin tone!

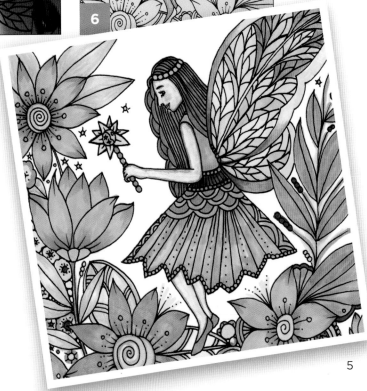

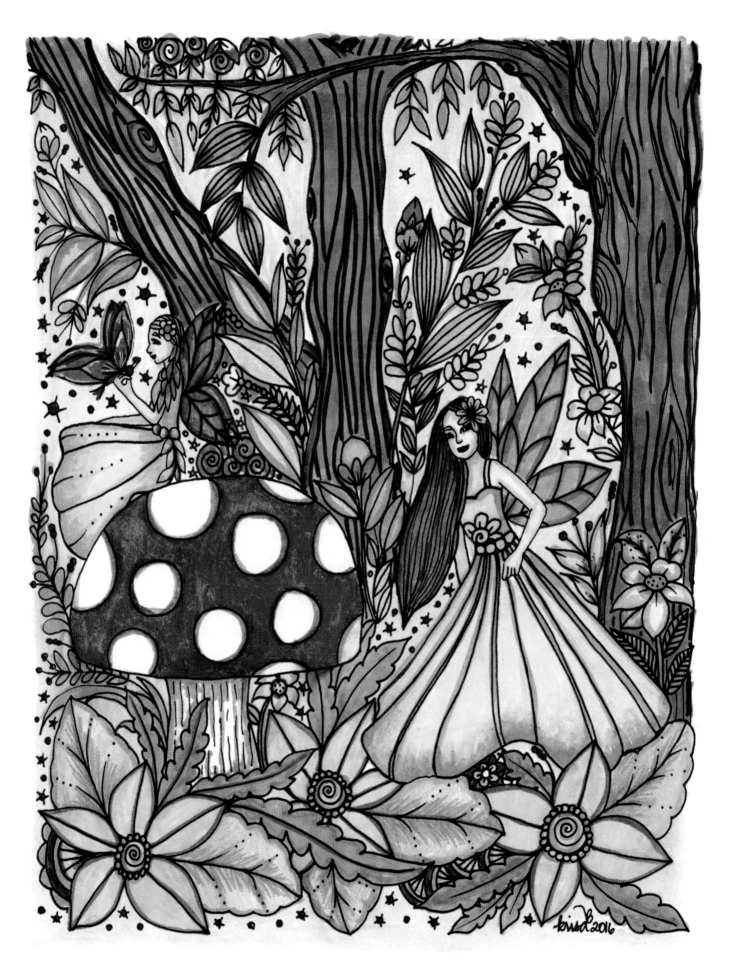

*Mushroom Meeting Place, page 39.*

*Markers (Copic, Winsor & Newton), water-soluble pastels (Caran d'Ache). Color by Krisa Bousquet.*

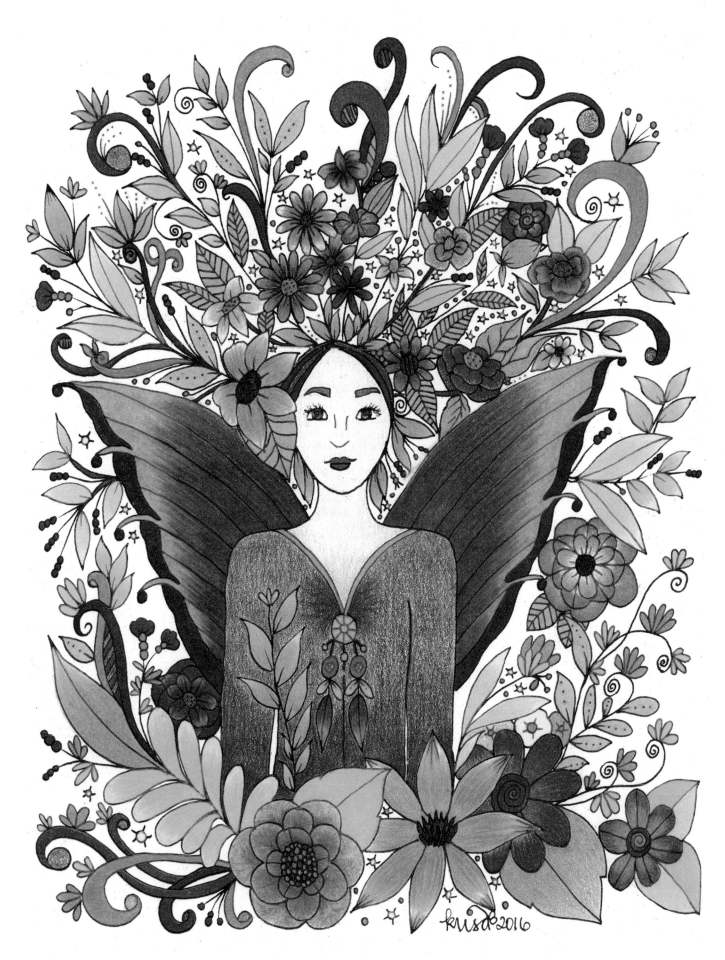

*Blossoming Hairdo, page 45.*
*Colored pencils (Prismacolor). Color by Heather Gibson.*

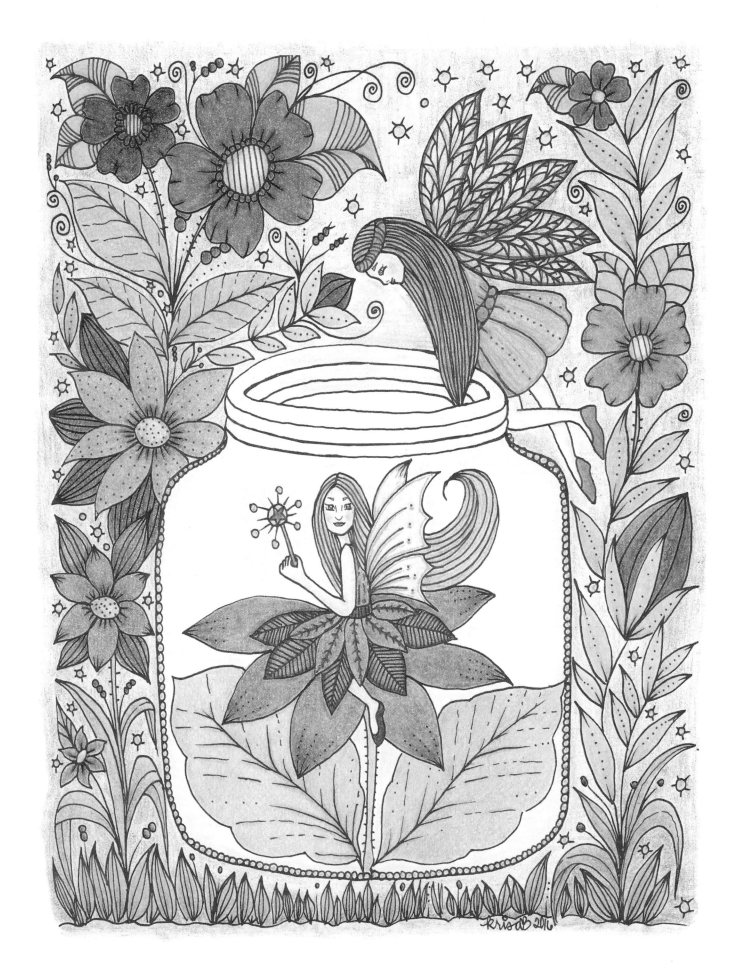

*The Fairy Jar, page 35.*

*Colored pencils (Prismacolor), gel pens (Sakura). Color by Annie Jump.*

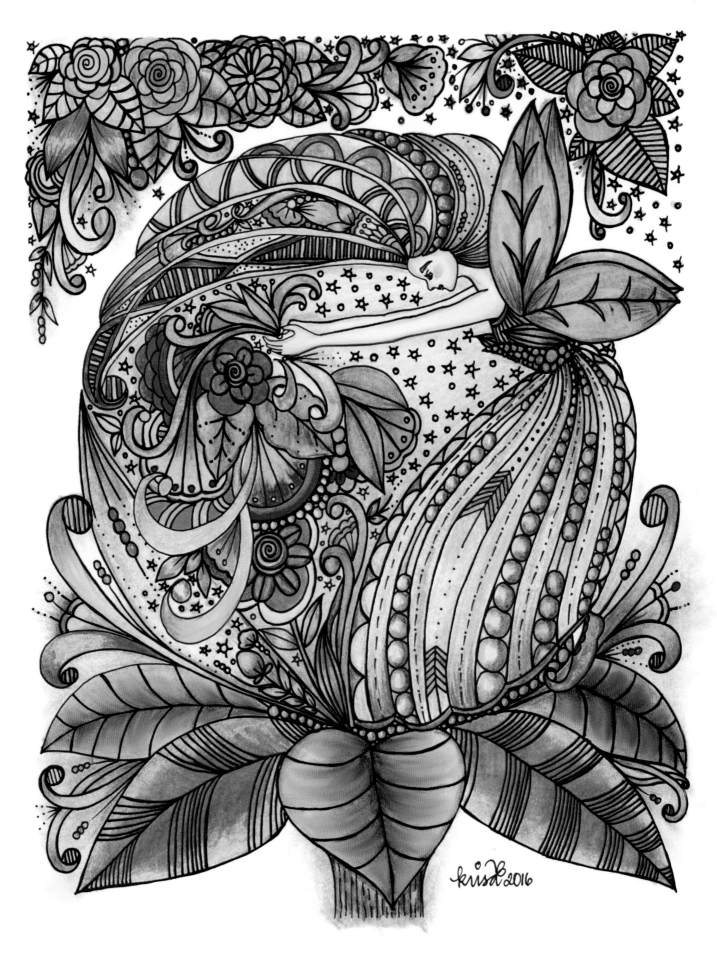

*Magical Orb, page 73.*
*Markers (Blick), colored pencils (Prismacolor). Color by Krisa Bousquet.*

9

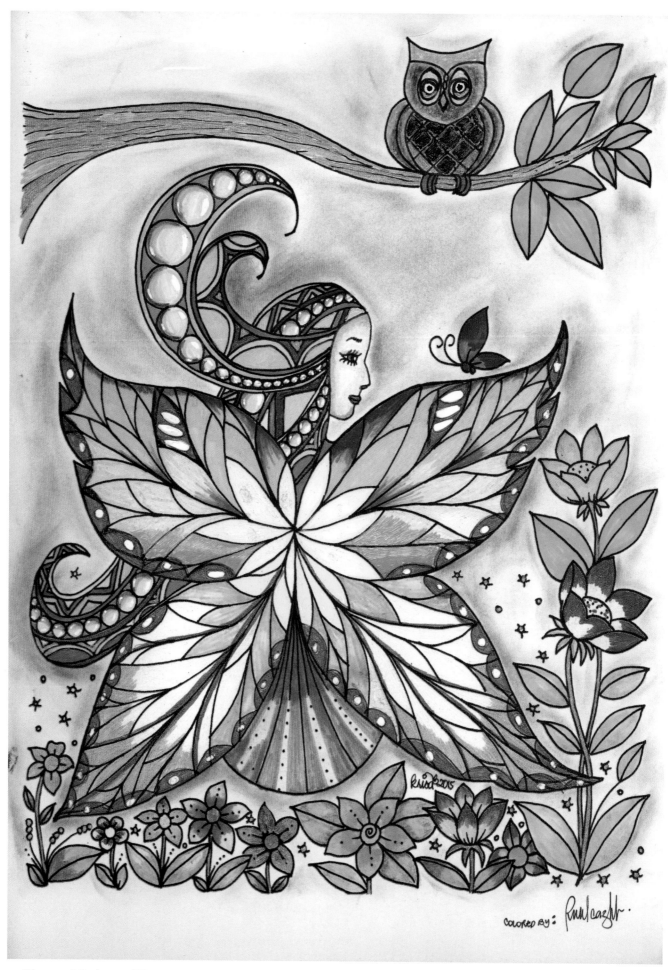

*Observant Owl, page 33.*

*Colored pencils (Prismacolor), gel pens. Color by Razell Alcazar.*

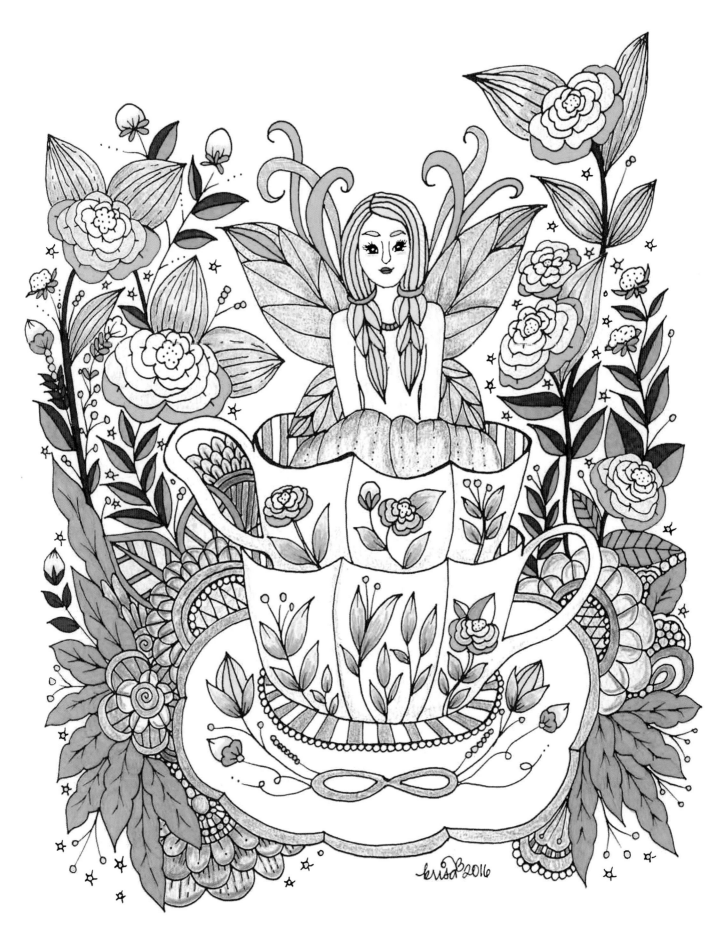

*Tea Time, page 47.*
*Colored pencils, markers. Color by Layla Montagne.*     11

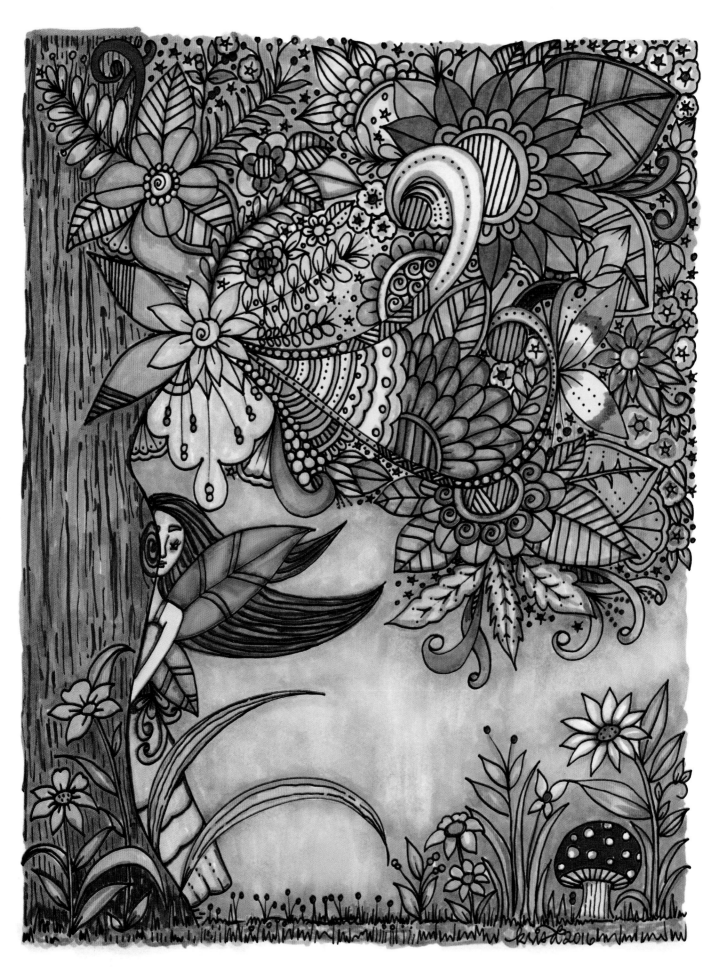

*Peekaboo, page 41.*

*Markers (Conda), colored pencils (Prismacolor). Color by Krisa Bousquet.*

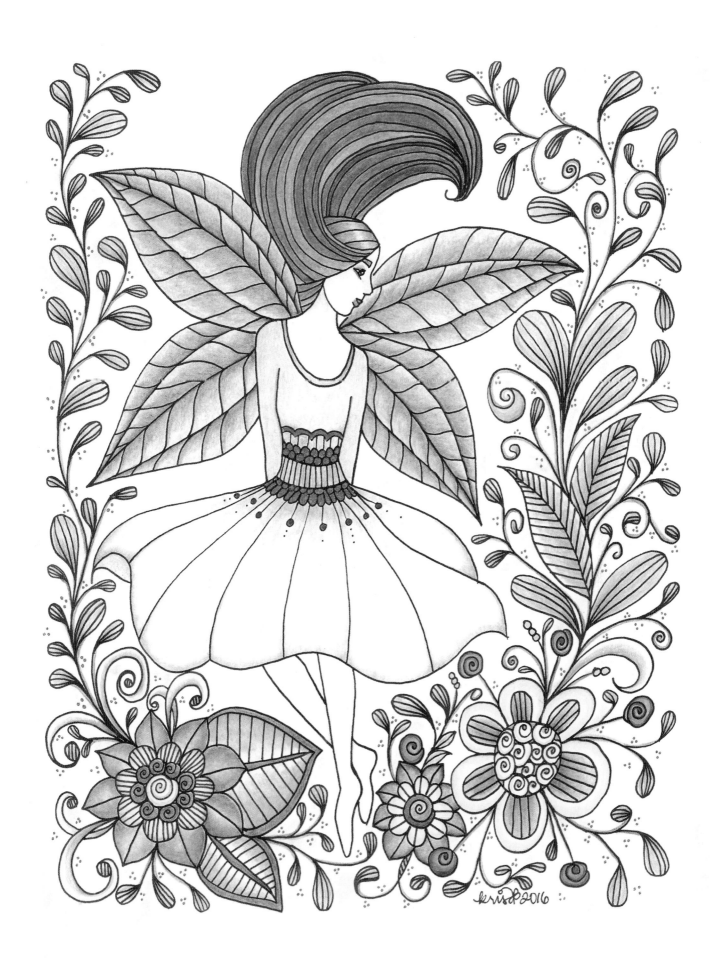

*Dancing in the Vines, page 37.*
*Colored pencils (Faber-Castell), watercolor pencils (Derwent), markers, gel pens, pastels. Color by Lisa Caryl.*

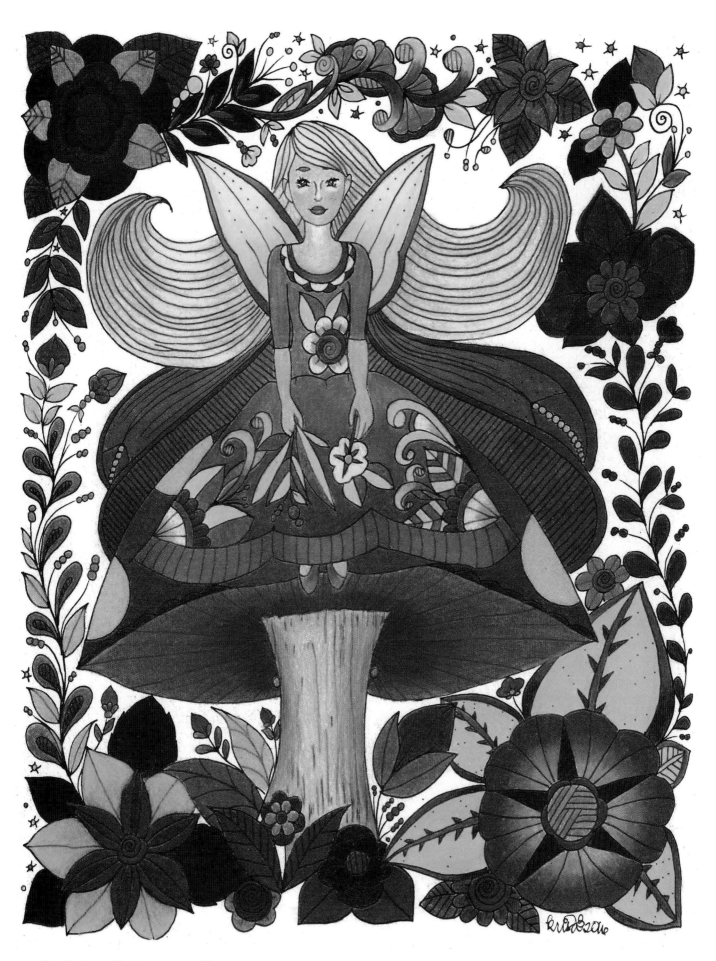

*Perched on a Mushroom, page 71.*

14    *Colored pencils. Color by Rachel Simpson.*

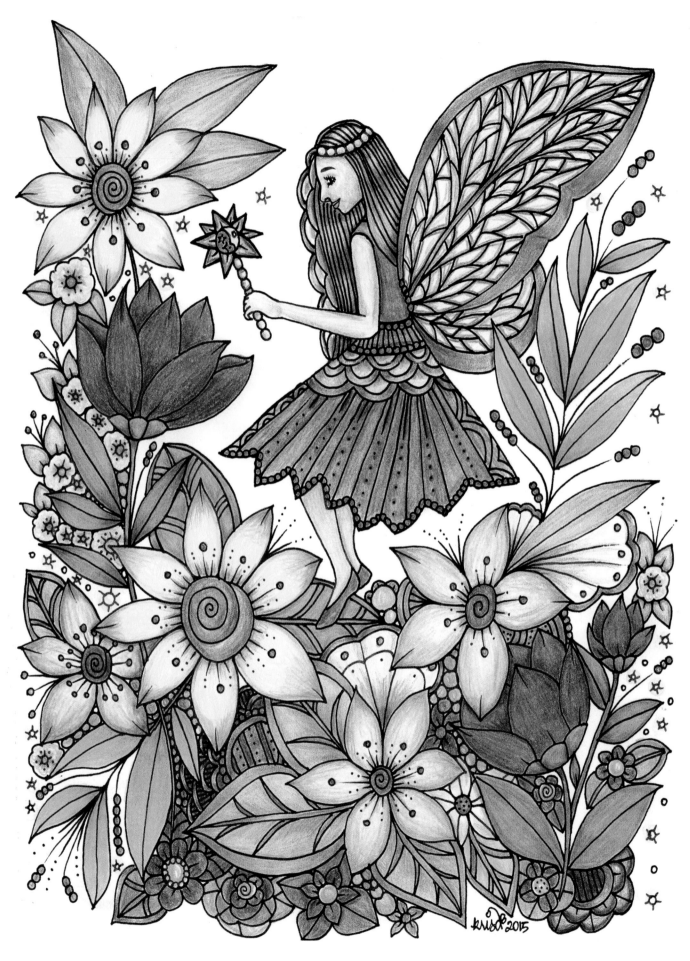

*Enchanting the Flowers, page 43.*
*Colored pencils (Faber-Castell). Color by Laura Brumby.* 15

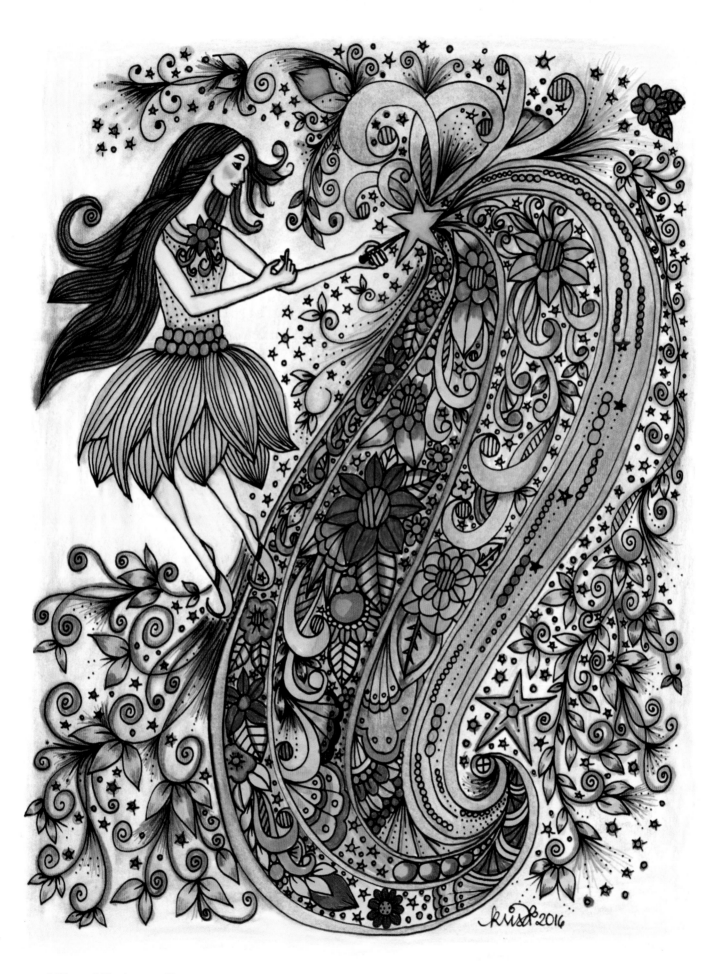

*A Wave of Magic, page 17.*

16    *Markers (Conda), colored pencils (Prismacolor). Color by Krisa Bousquet.*

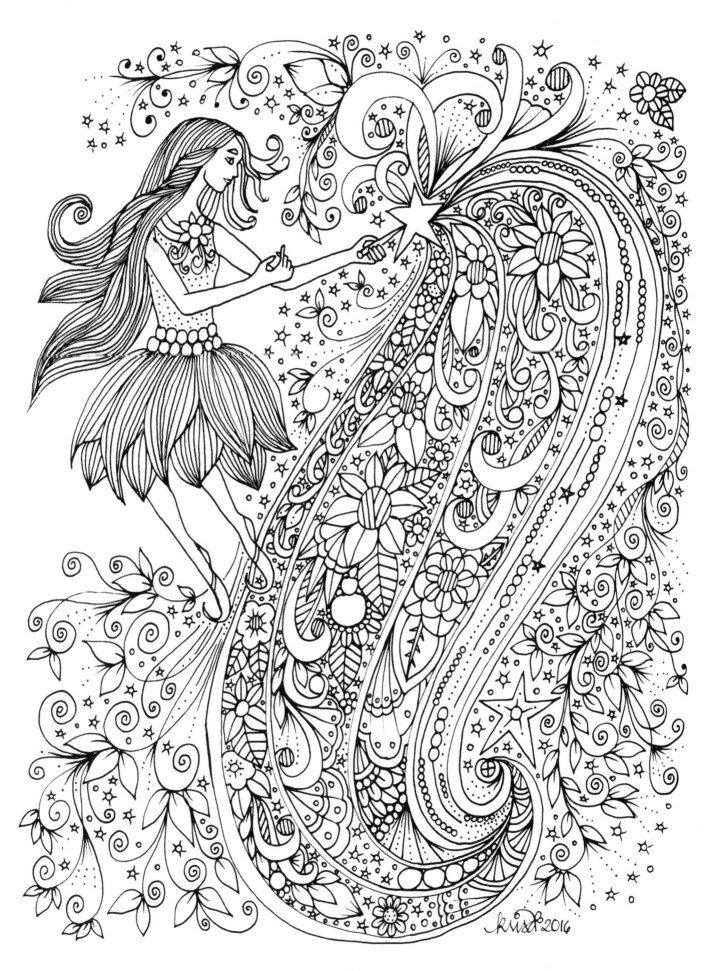

17

Leave room in your garden
for fairies to dance.

—Unknown

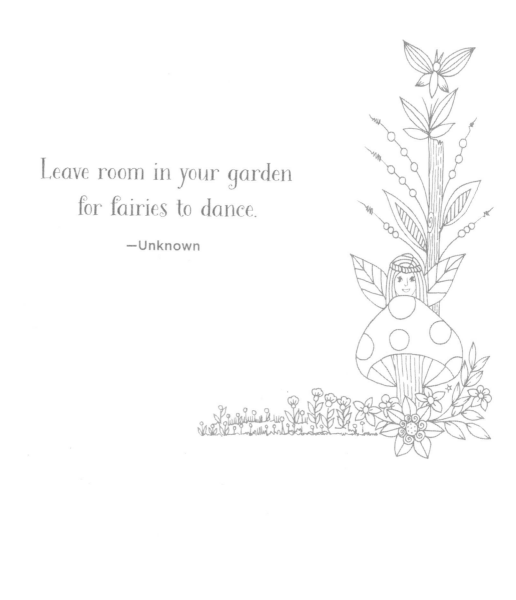

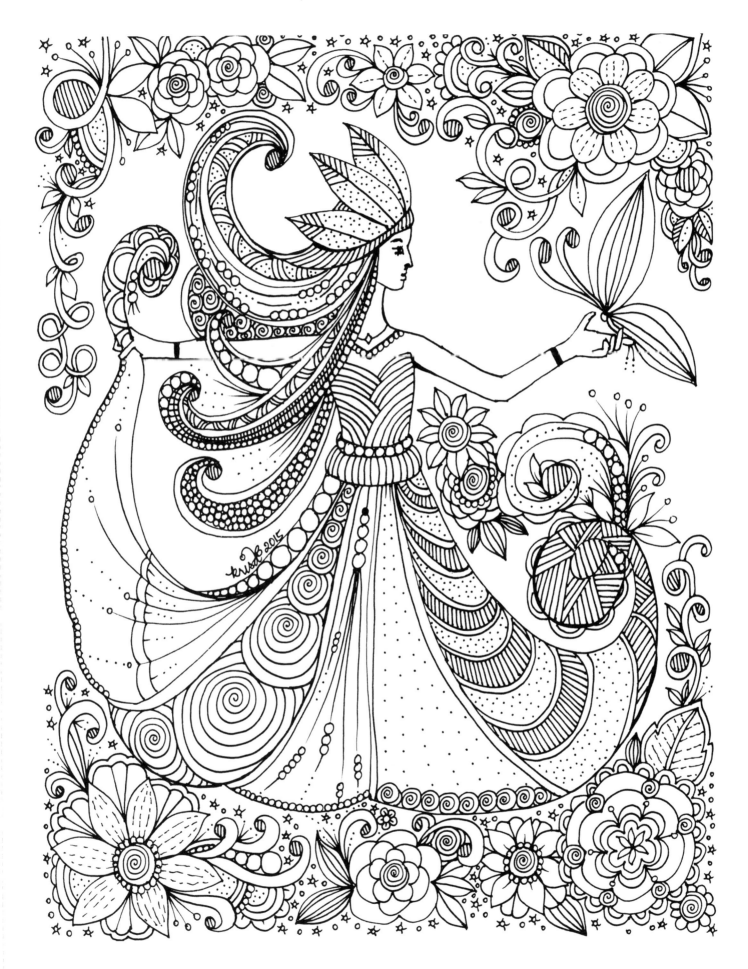

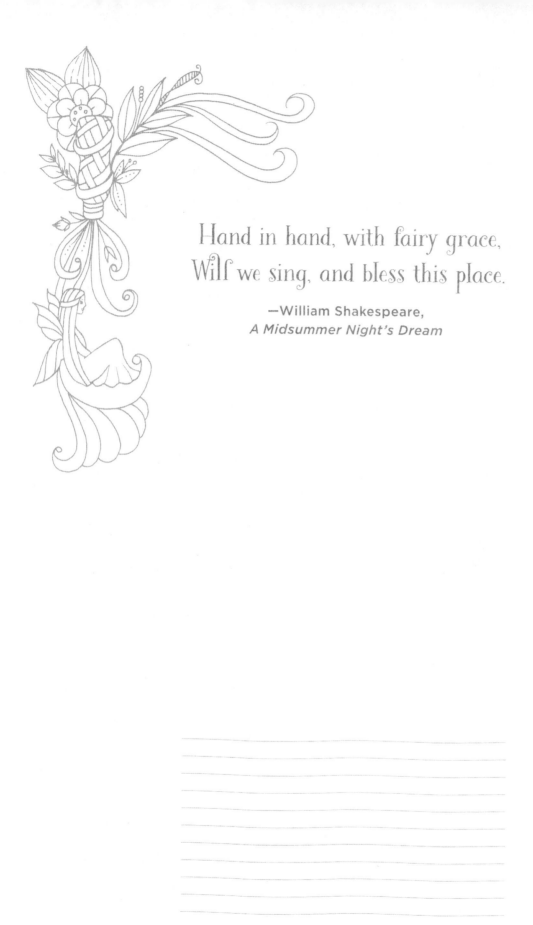

Hand in hand, with fairy grace,
Will we sing, and bless this place.

—William Shakespeare,
*A Midsummer Night's Dream*

**The Fairy Queen**

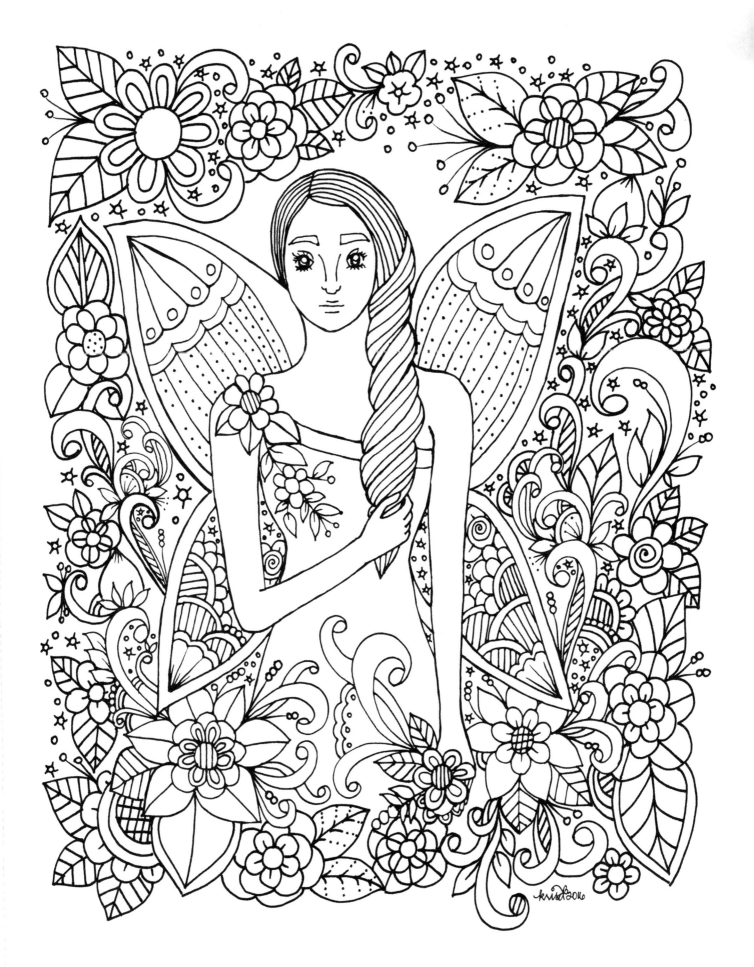

21

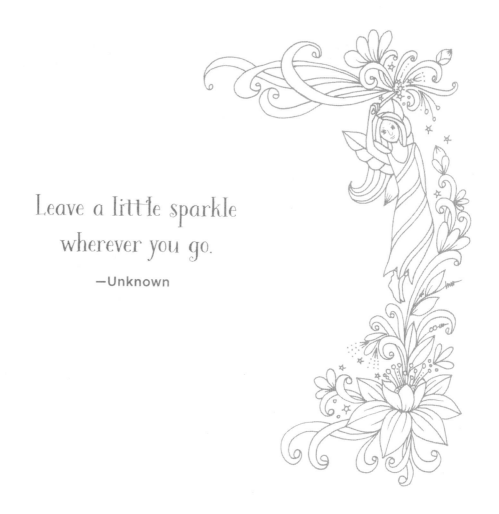

Leave a little sparkle
wherever you go.

—Unknown

_____
_____
_____
_____
_____
_____
_____
_____
_____
_____

**Nestled in the Flowers**

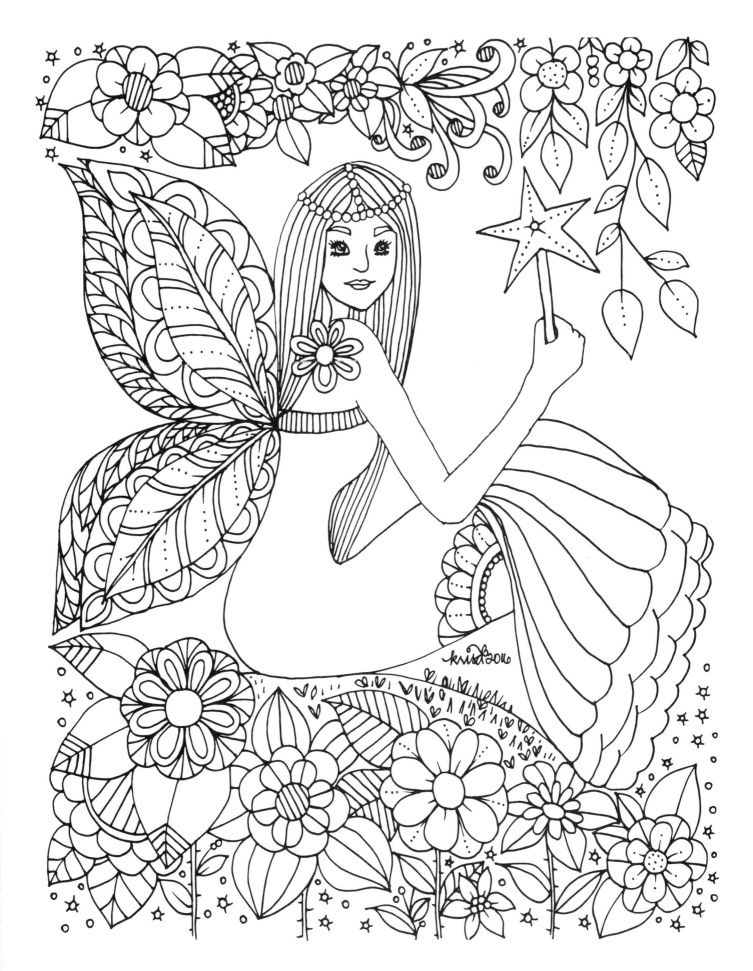

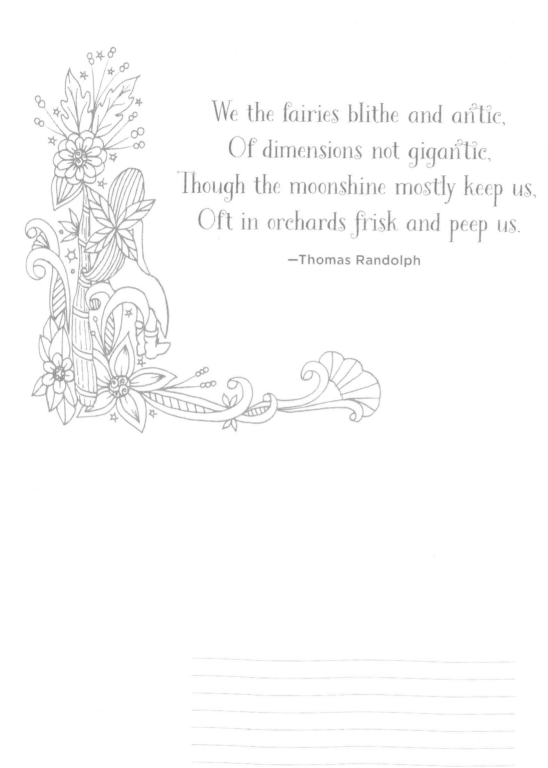

We the fairies blithe and antic,
Of dimensions not gigantic,
Though the moonshine mostly keep us,
Oft in orchards frisk and peep us.

—Thomas Randolph

_____
_____
_____
_____
_____
_____
_____
_____
_____

**The Star Wand**

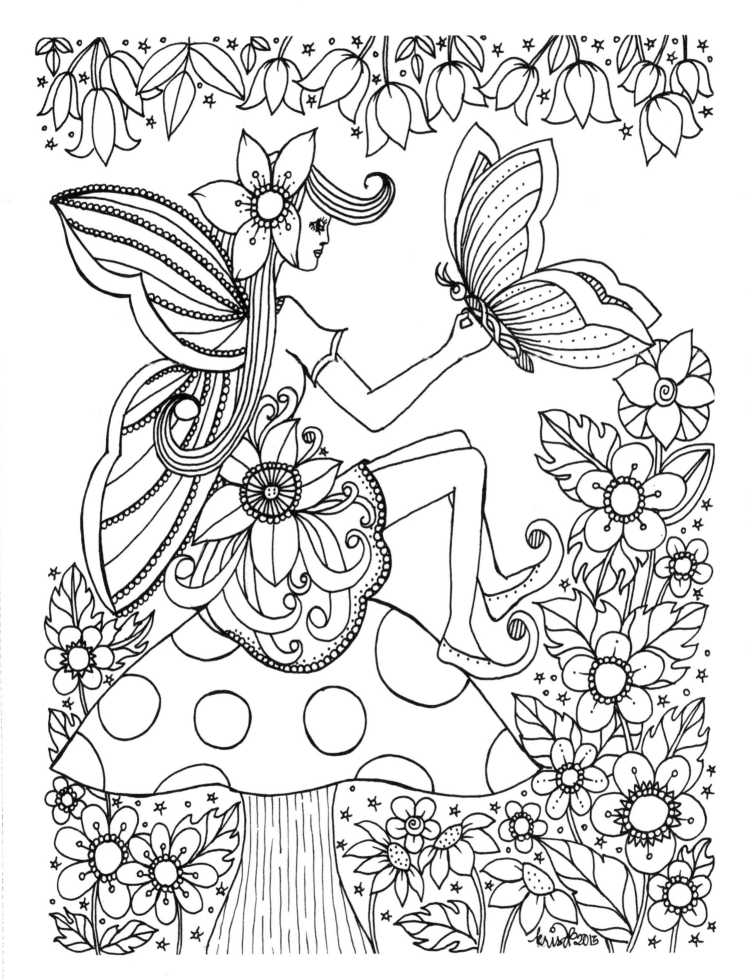

Nothing can be truer than fairy wisdom.
It is as true as sunbeams.

—Douglas William Jerrold

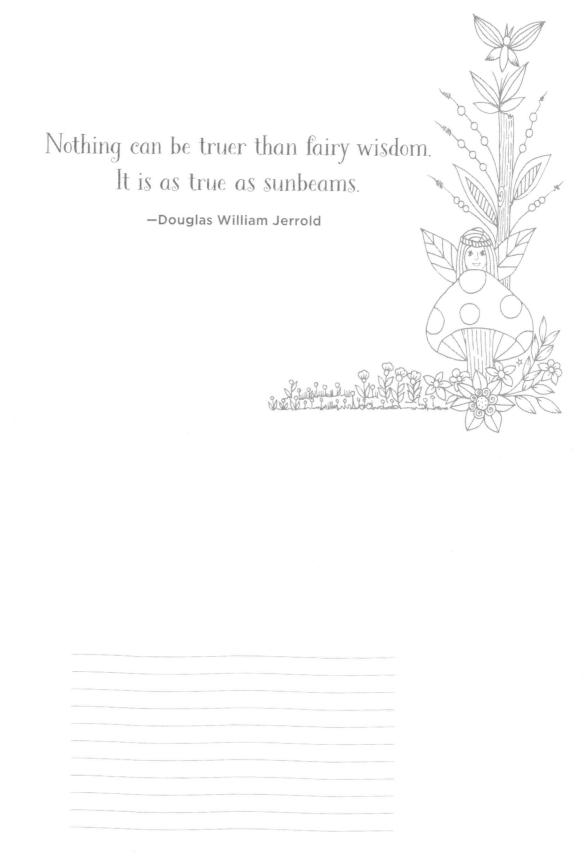

_____
_____
_____
_____
_____
_____
_____
_____
_____

**Butterfly Visitor**

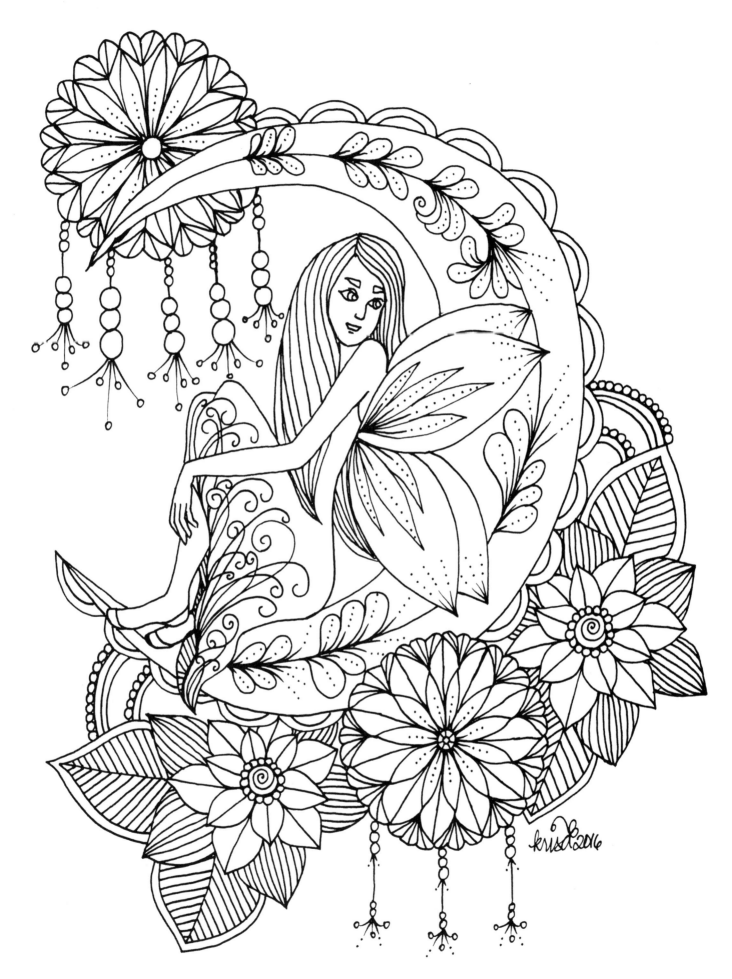

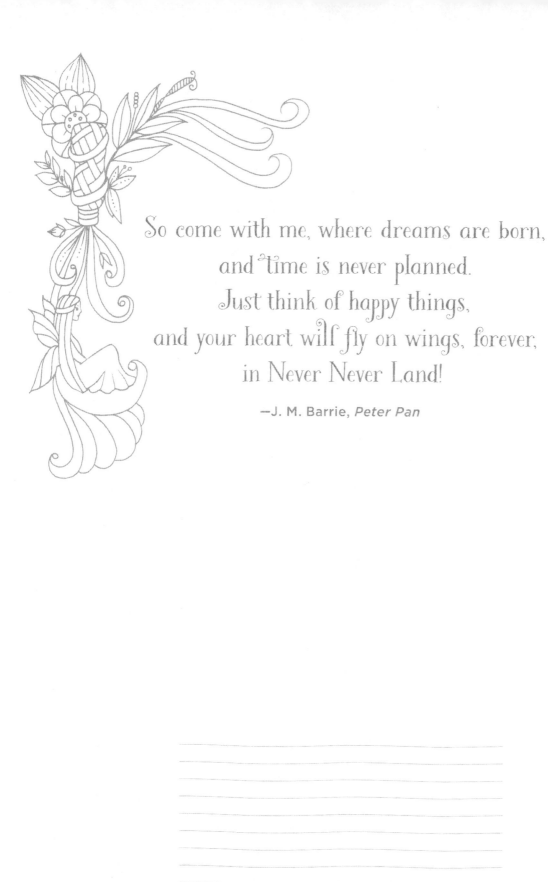

So come with me, where dreams are born,
and time is never planned.
Just think of happy things,
and your heart will fly on wings, forever,
in Never Never Land!

—J. M. Barrie, *Peter Pan*

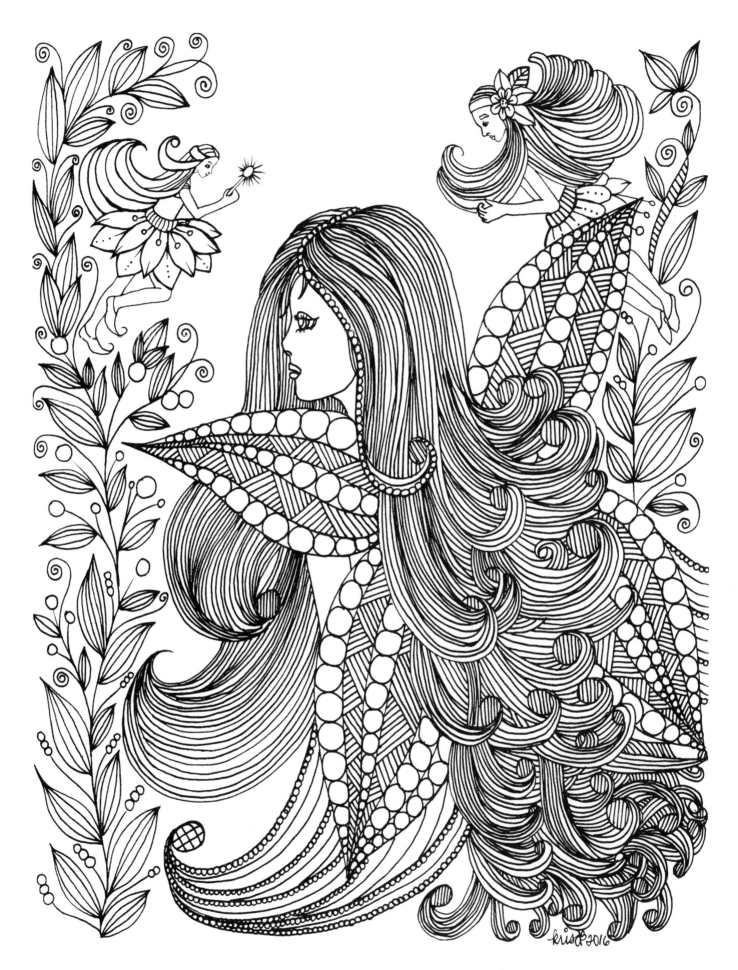

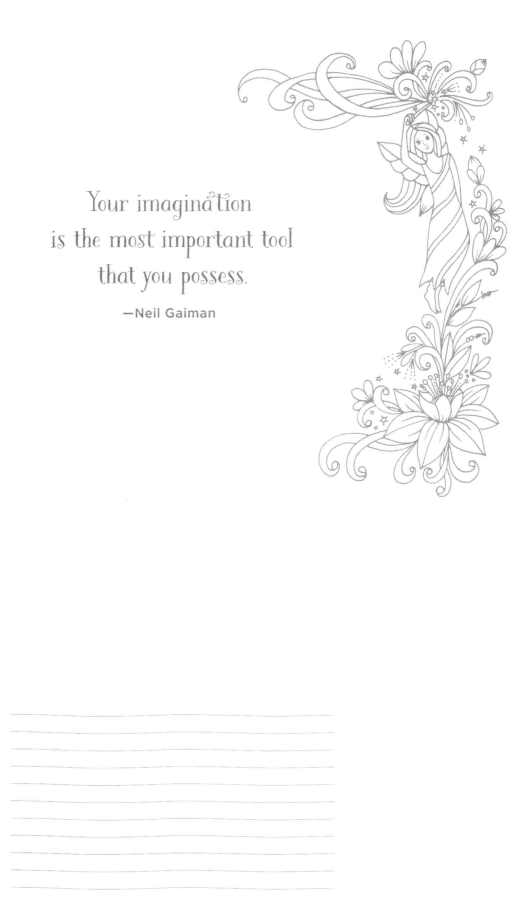

Your imagination
is the most important tool
that you possess.

—Neil Gaiman

Fairy Curls

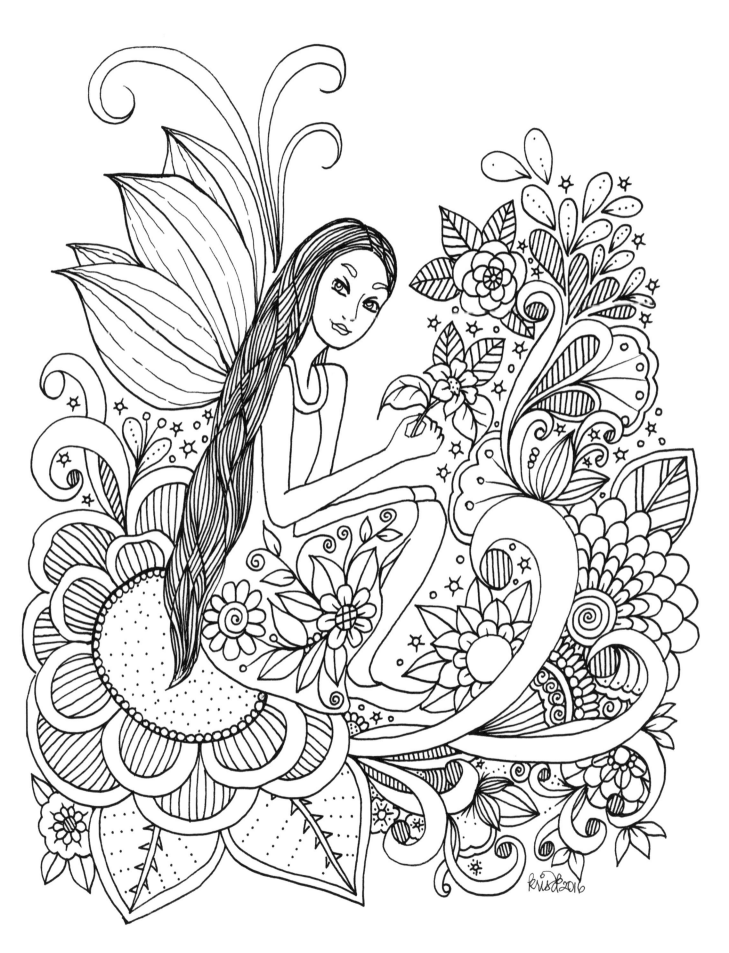

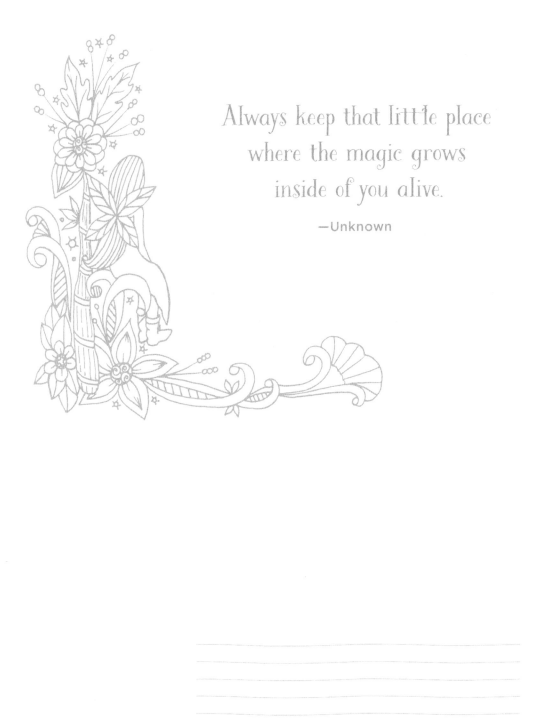

Always keep that little place
where the magic grows
inside of you alive.

—Unknown

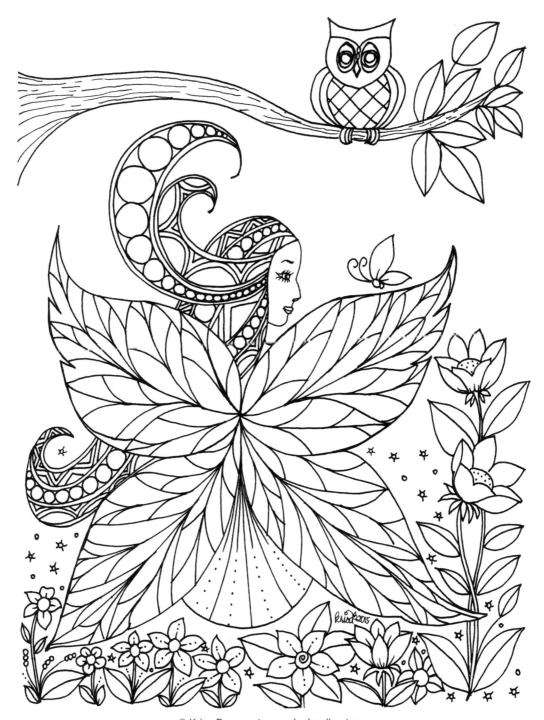

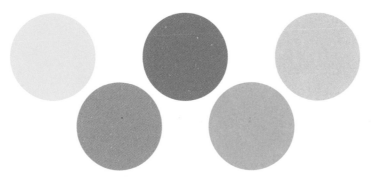

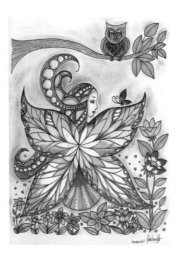

Try coloring a pair of fairy wings in all warm colors,
going from light yellow to dark red for a fantastic ombré.

How dreary the world would be
if there were no fairies.

—Unknown

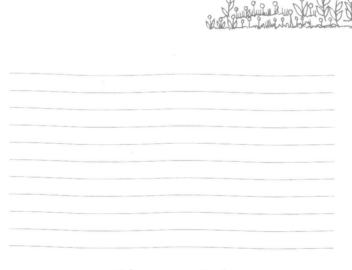

**Observant Owl**

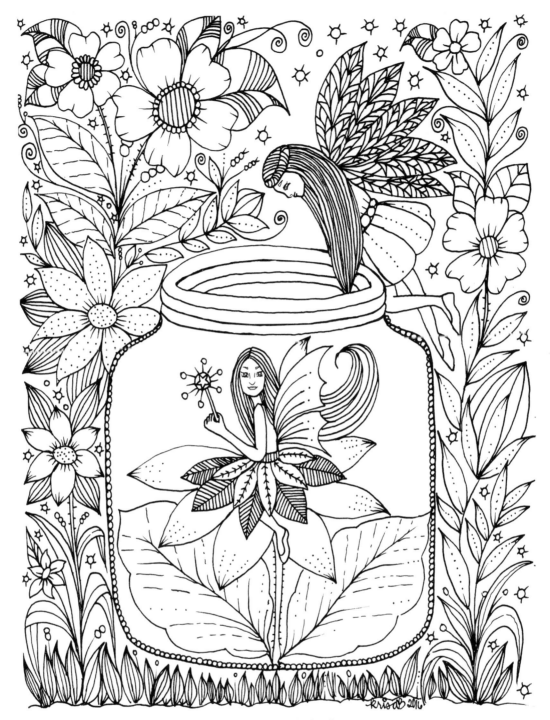

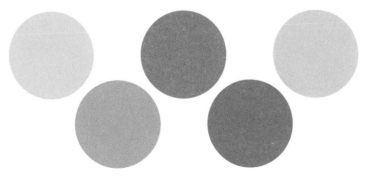

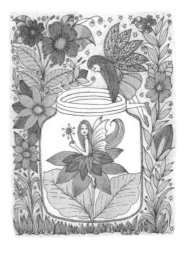

On a light, cool green and blue background, a few touches of bright, warm colors will really pop, like the red and purple here.

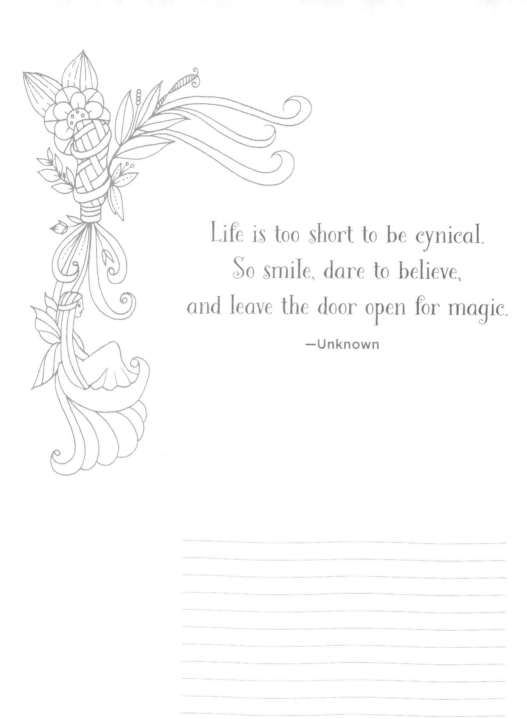

Life is too short to be cynical.
So smile, dare to believe,
and leave the door open for magic.

—Unknown

The Fairy Jar

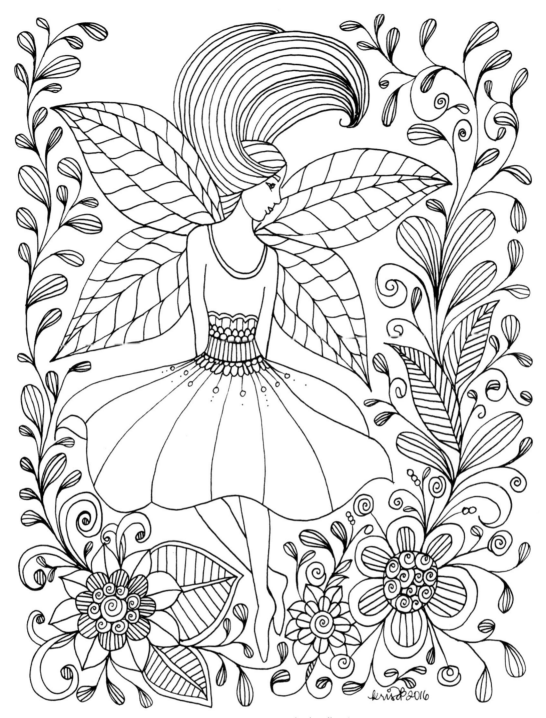

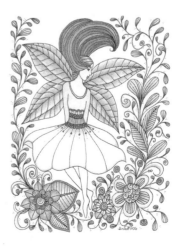

Even with a mix of different colors,
you can achieve a very soft, muted look by using light pressure
and thoroughly blending your shades.

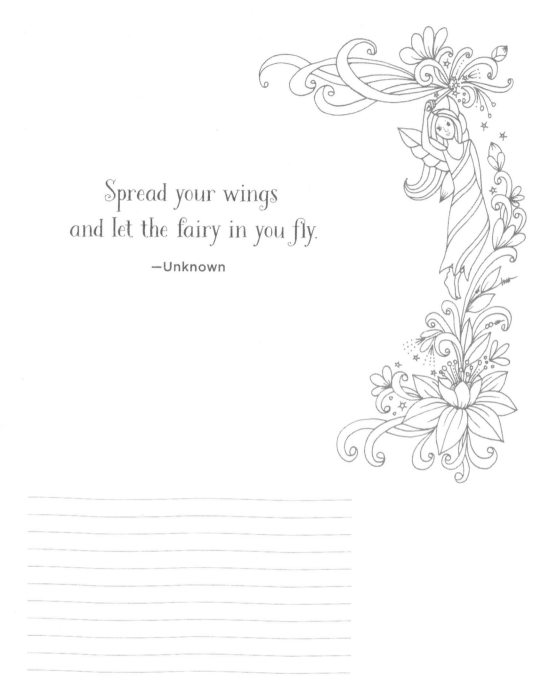

Spread your wings
and let the fairy in you fly.

—Unknown

_____
_____
_____
_____
_____
_____
_____
_____
_____
_____

**Dancing in the Vines**

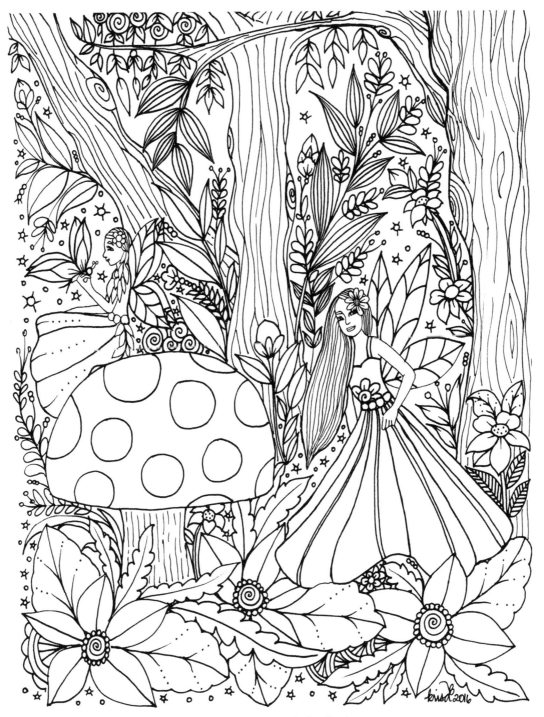

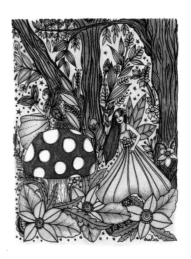

Don't feel like you have to be fancy with lots of special colors!
Get back to basics by mixing intense primary colors
with a neutral like brown.

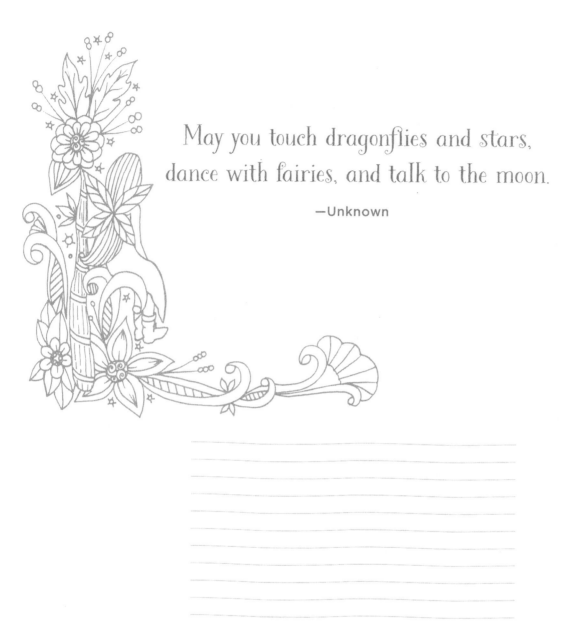

May you touch dragonflies and stars,
dance with fairies, and talk to the moon.

—Unknown

**Mushroom Meeting Place**

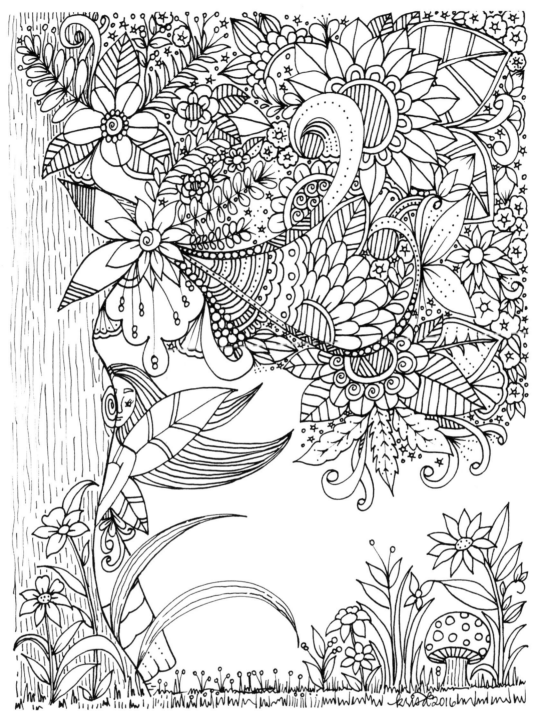

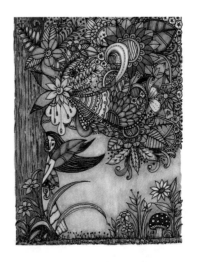

Mix natural and fantastical colors by using green as your dominant leaf color, but adding in some warm tones.

They say if you dream a thing
more than once, it's sure to come true.

*—Sleeping Beauty*

_____
_____
_____
_____
_____
_____
_____
_____
_____
_____

**Peekaboo**

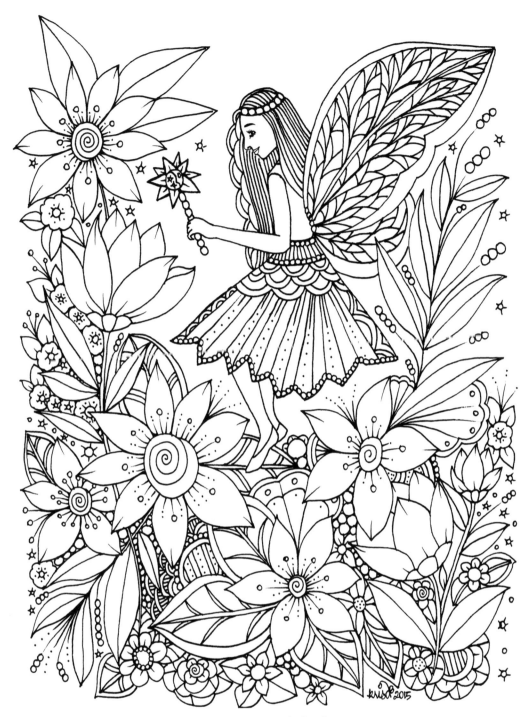

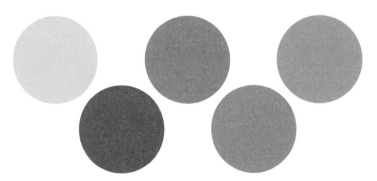

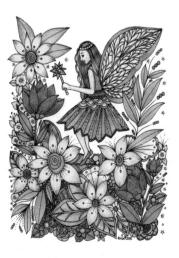

You can always add a color background to a piece of art,
but it's also nice to keep the background white, because then
every shape and color really stands out.

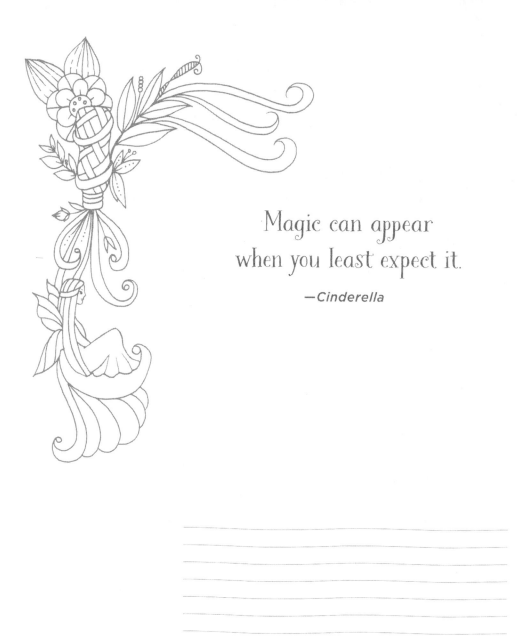

Magic can appear
when you least expect it.

*—Cinderella*

**Enchanting the Flowers**

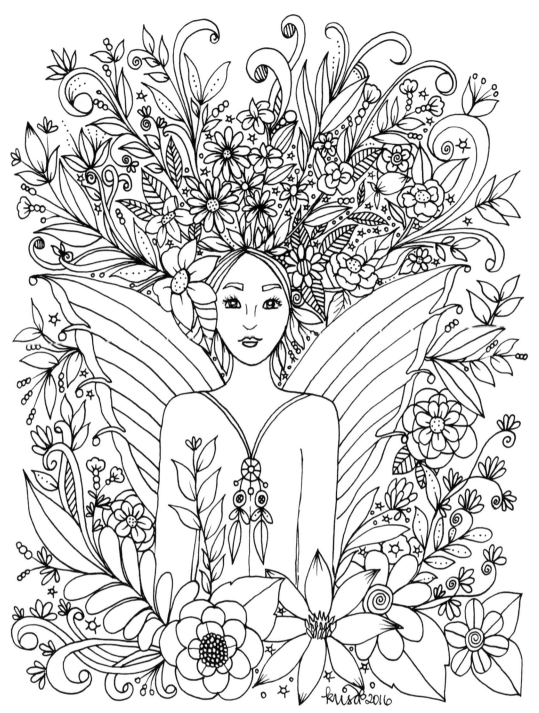

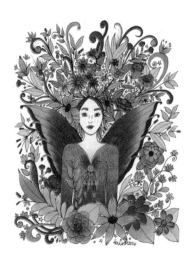

One way to get started on a design is to color the central motif with many shades of one color. Then surround it with a totally different color for solid contrast.

In the midst of our lives,
we must find the magic that makes
our souls soar.

—Unknown

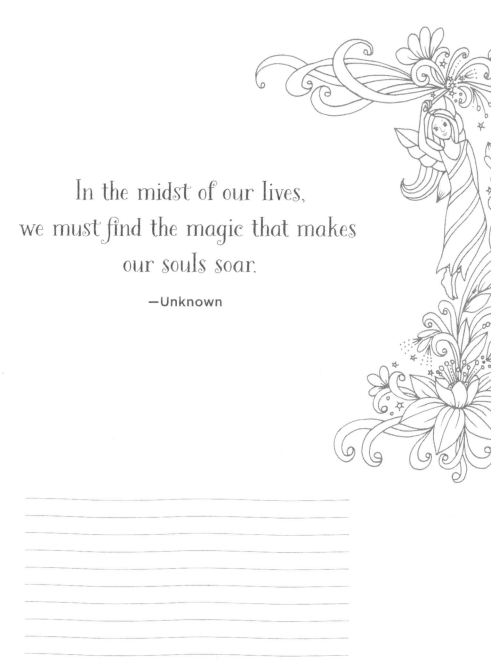

_____
_____
_____
_____
_____
_____
_____
_____
_____
_____

**Blossoming Hairdo**

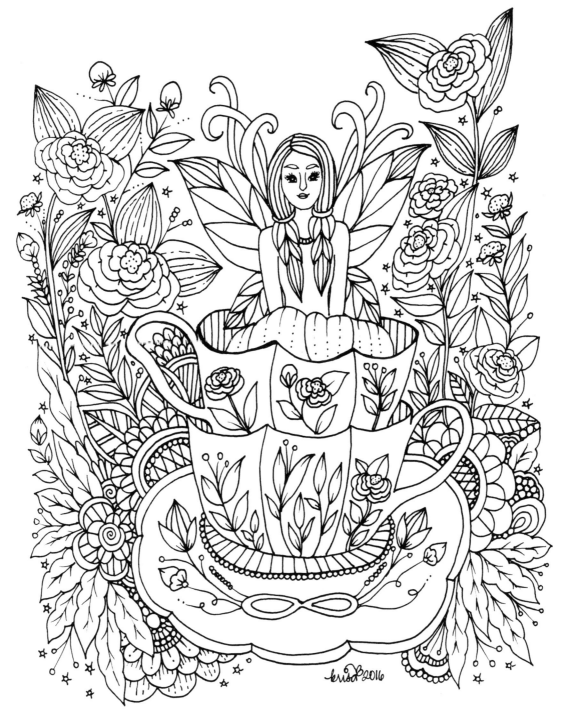

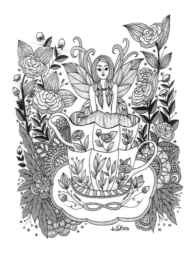

You can leave areas of a design white, as well as the background,
to create a minimalist but still stunning coloring.

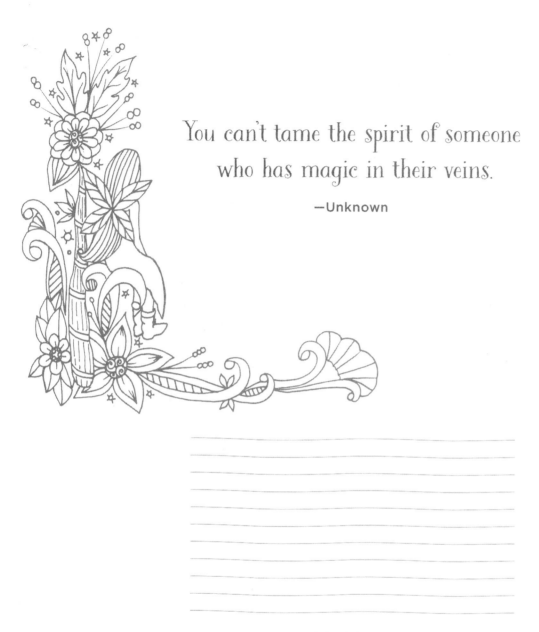

You can't tame the spirit of someone
who has magic in their veins.

—Unknown

_____
_____
_____
_____
_____
_____
_____
_____
_____
_____
_____

**Tea Time**

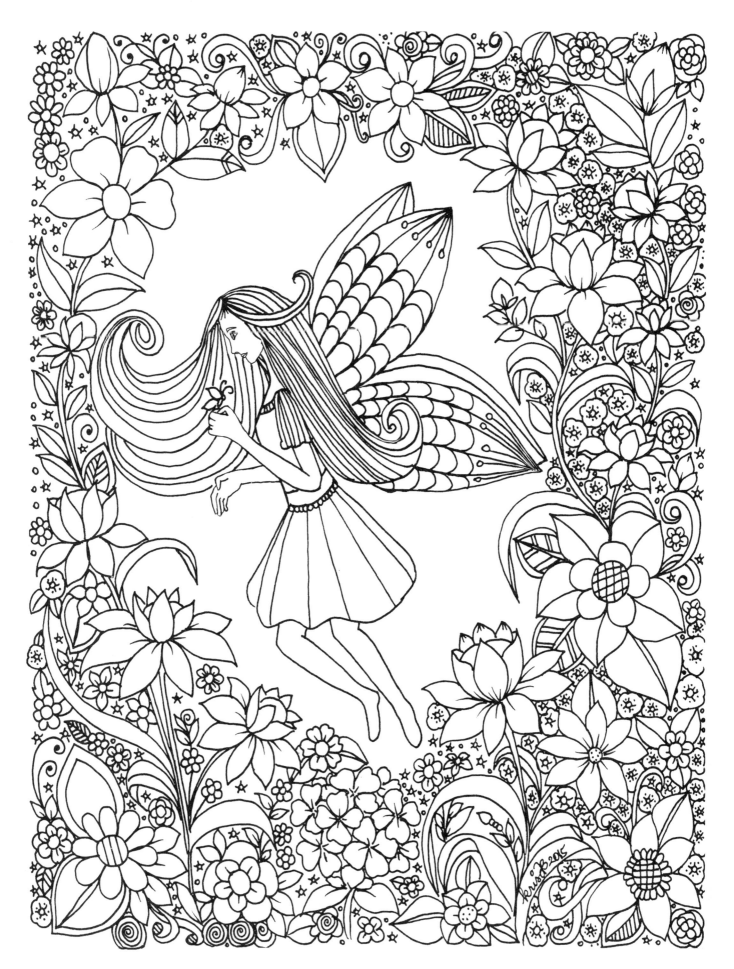

Fairies glitter my heart with giggles.

—Terri Guillemets

Fluttering Friend

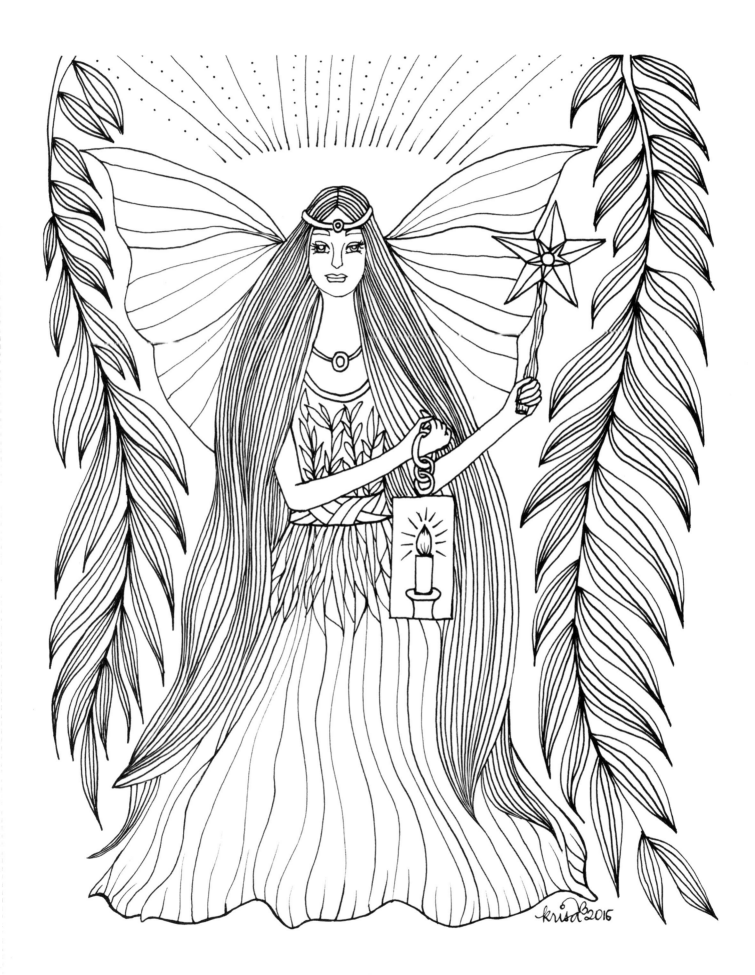

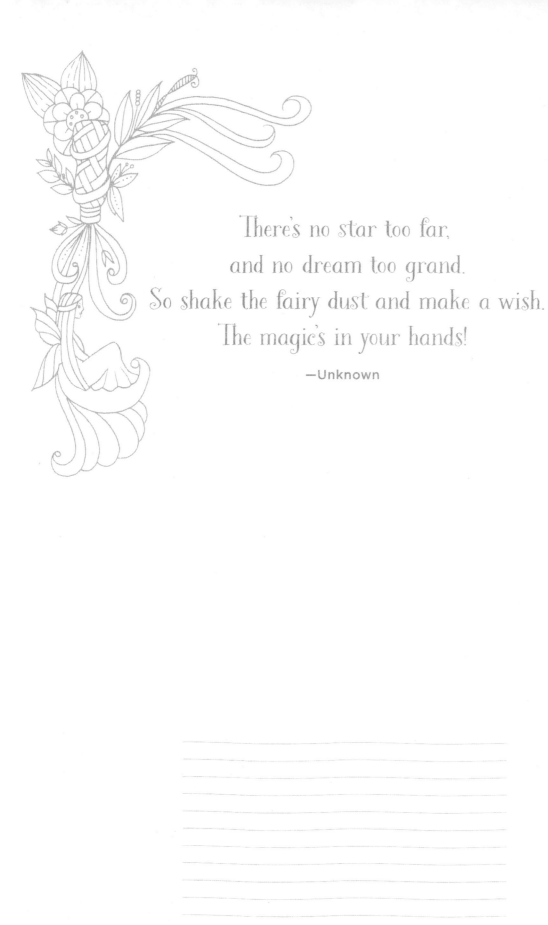

There's no star too far,
and no dream too grand.
So shake the fairy dust and make a wish.
The magic's in your hands!

—Unknown

**Lighting the Way**

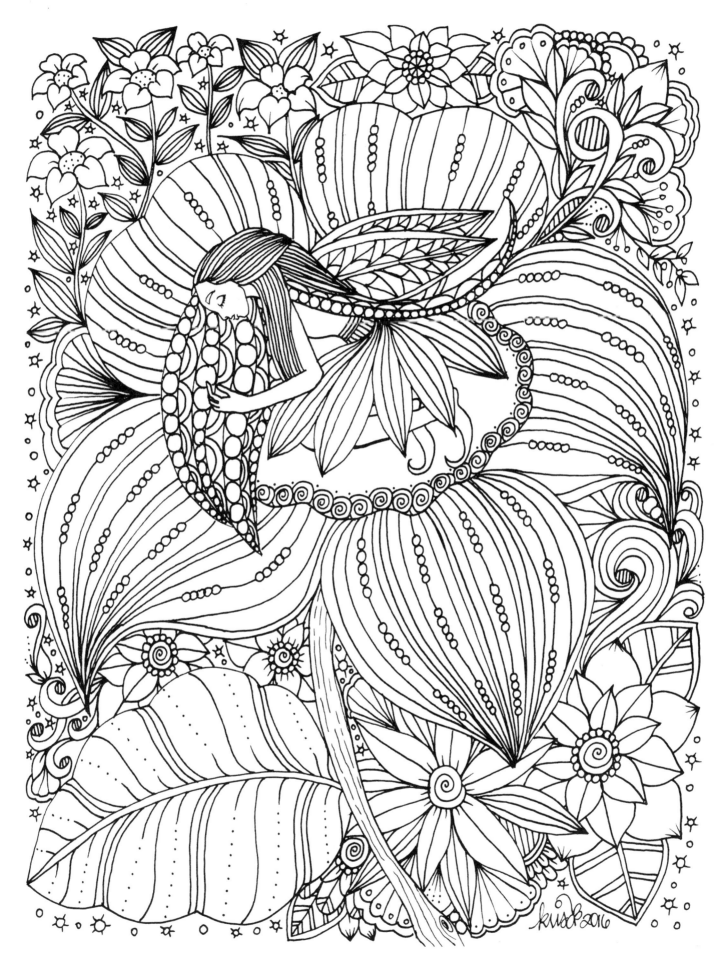

53

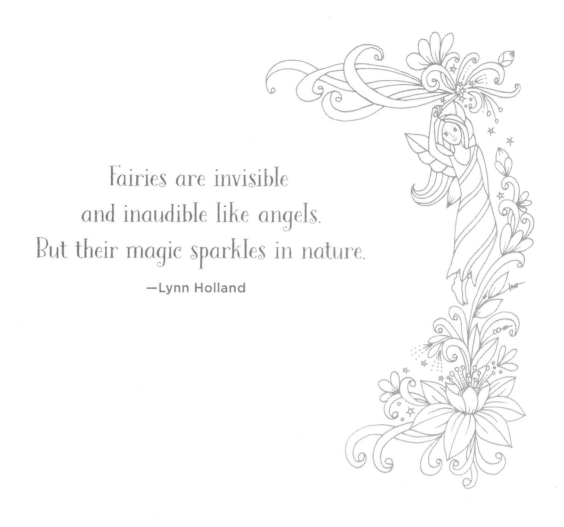

Fairies are invisible
and inaudible like angels.
But their magic sparkles in nature.

—Lynn Holland

_____
_____
_____
_____
_____
_____
_____

**Petal Bed**

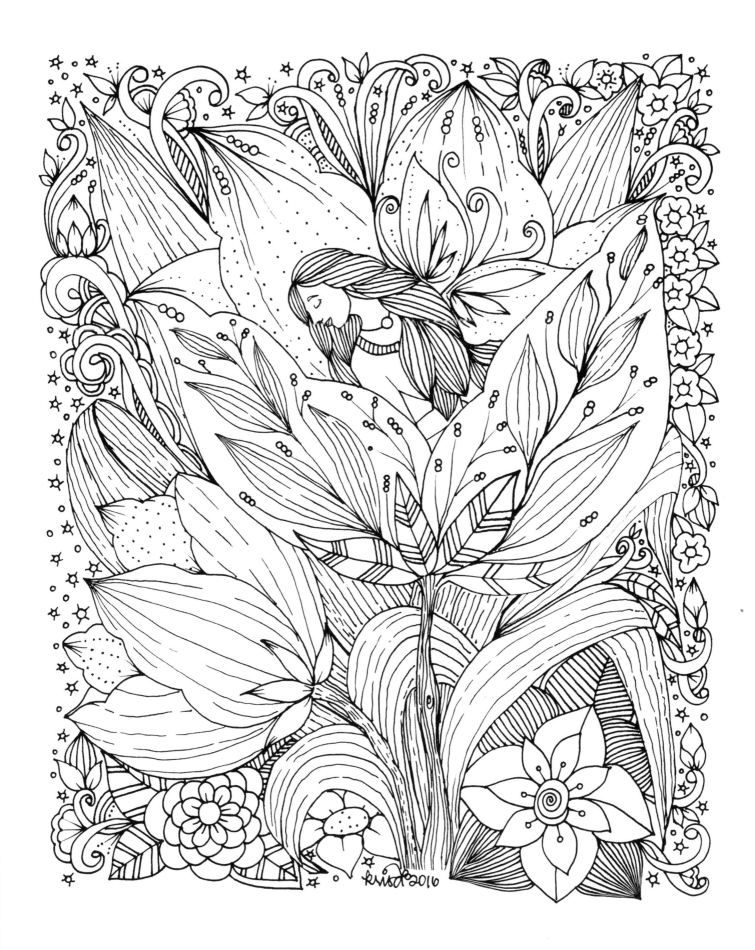

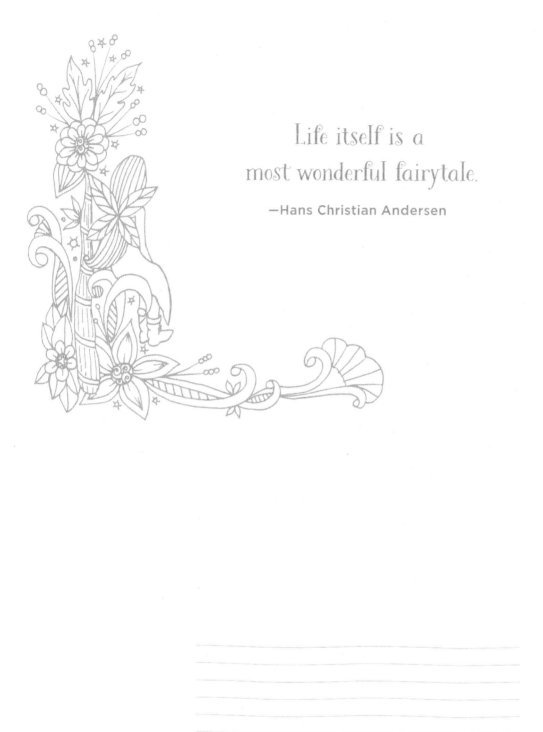

Life itself is a
most wonderful fairytale.

—Hans Christian Andersen

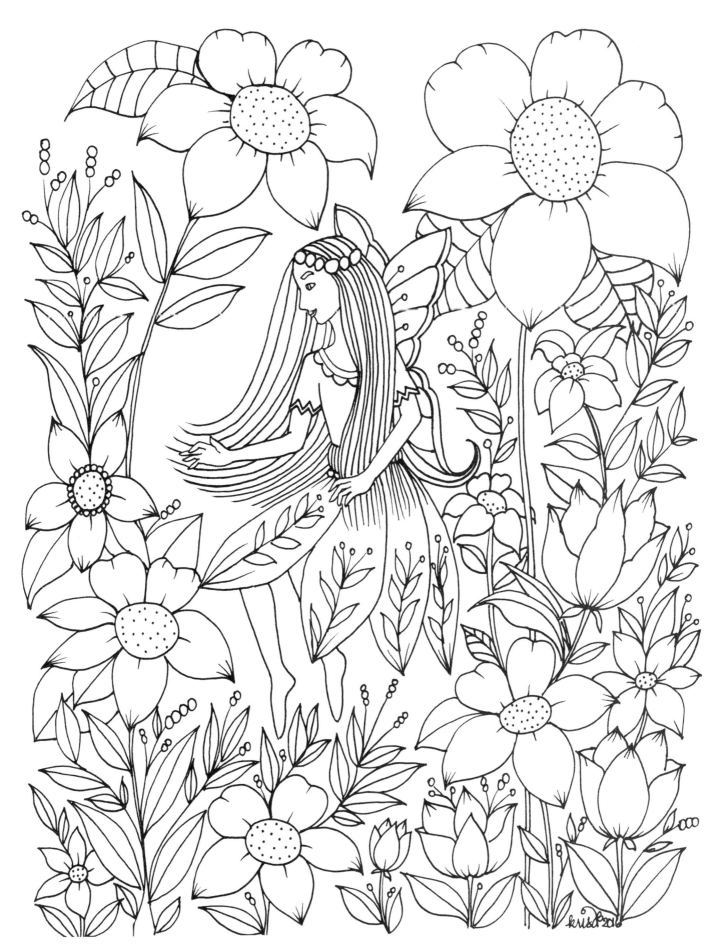

Where there is joy, laughter, and color, fairies will be found.

—Unknown

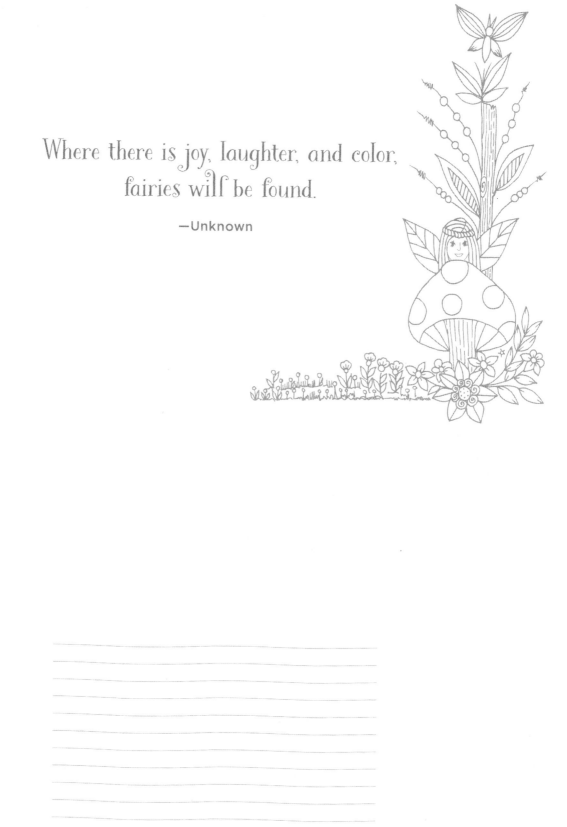

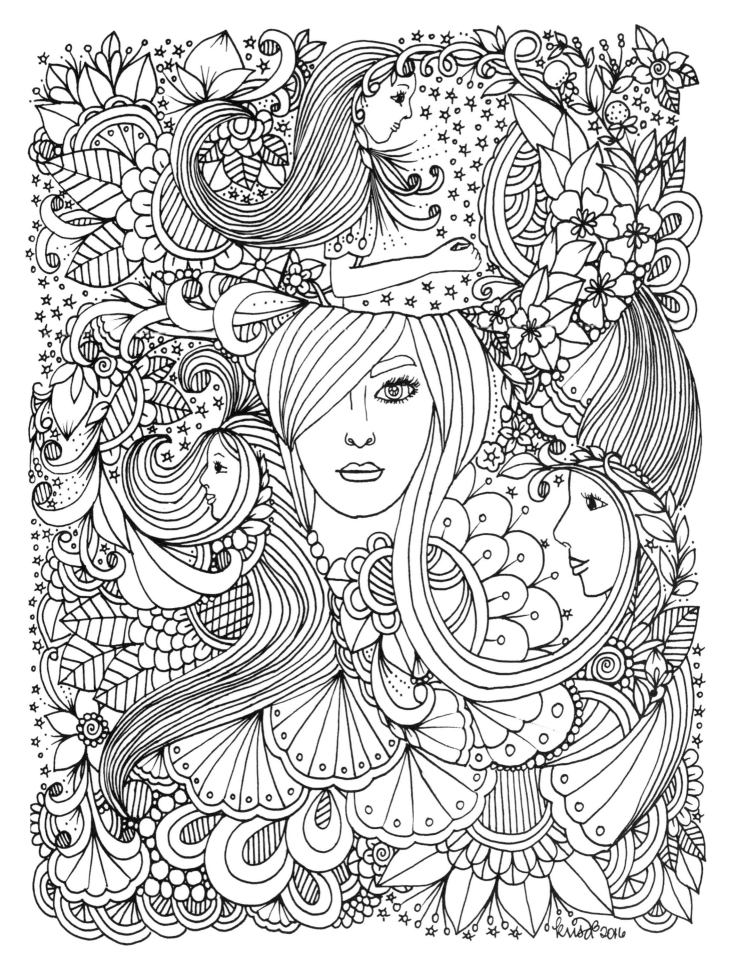

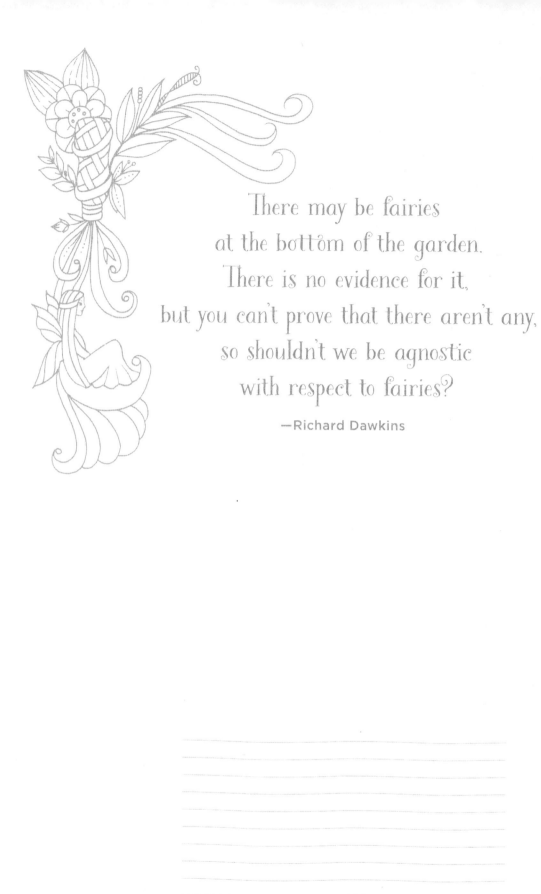

There may be fairies
at the bottom of the garden.
There is no evidence for it,
but you can't prove that there aren't any,
so shouldn't we be agnostic
with respect to fairies?

—Richard Dawkins

**Fairy Faces**

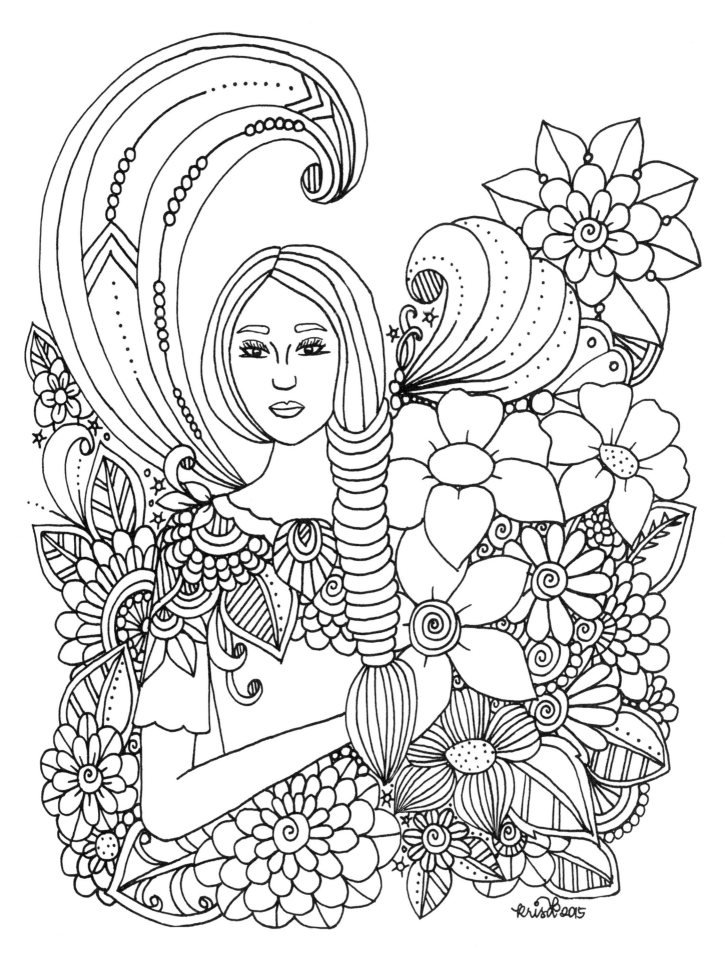

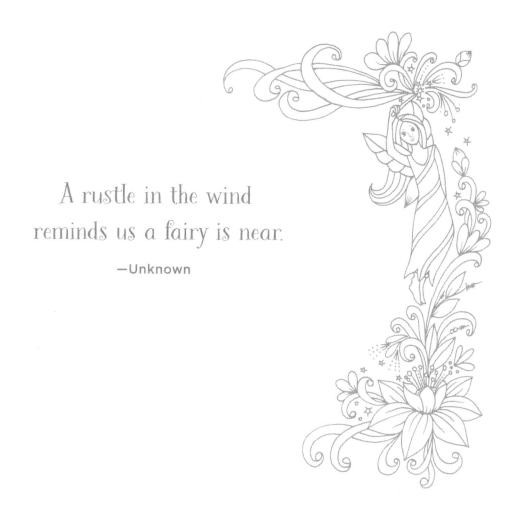

A rustle in the wind
reminds us a fairy is near.

—Unknown

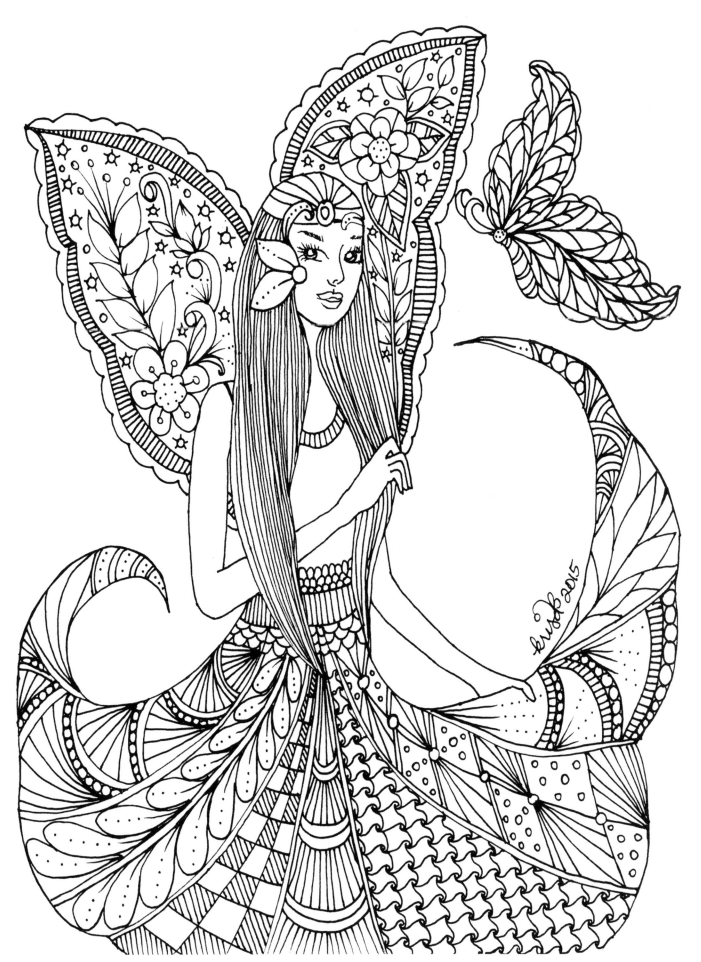

63

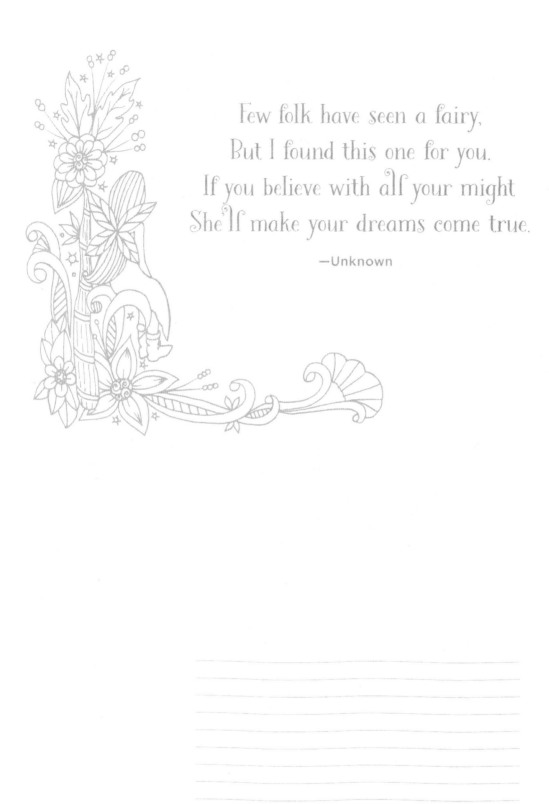

Few folk have seen a fairy,
But I found this one for you.
If you believe with all your might
She'll make your dreams come true.

—Unknown

A Hand-Sewn Skirt

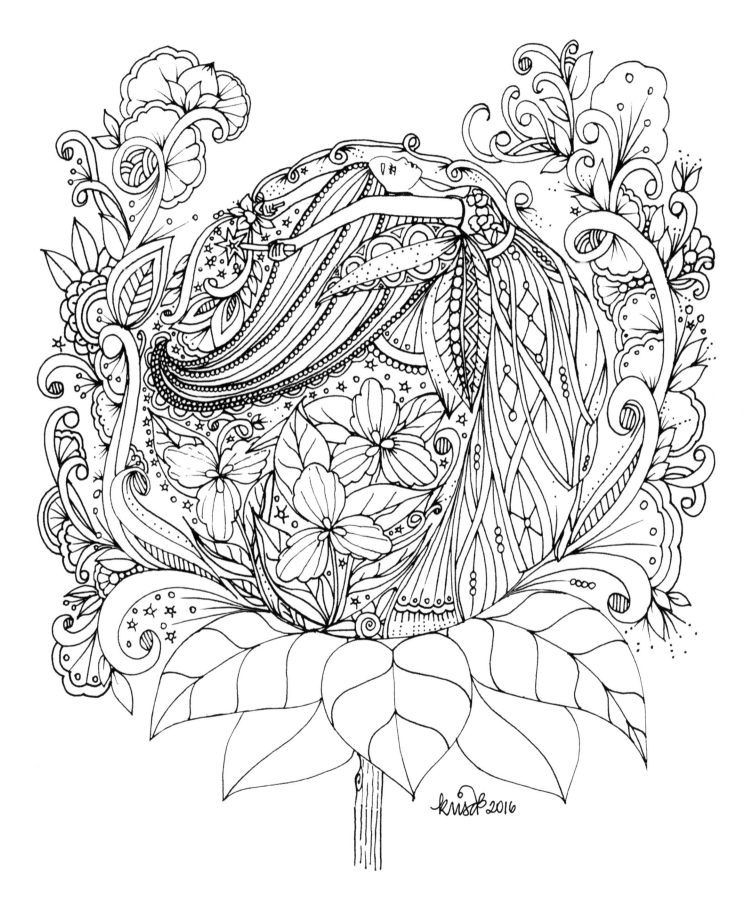

Faeries, come take me out of this dull world,
For I would ride with you upon the wind,
Run on the top of the disheveled tide,
And dance upon the mountains
like a flame.

—W. B. Yeats,
*The Land of Heart's Desire*

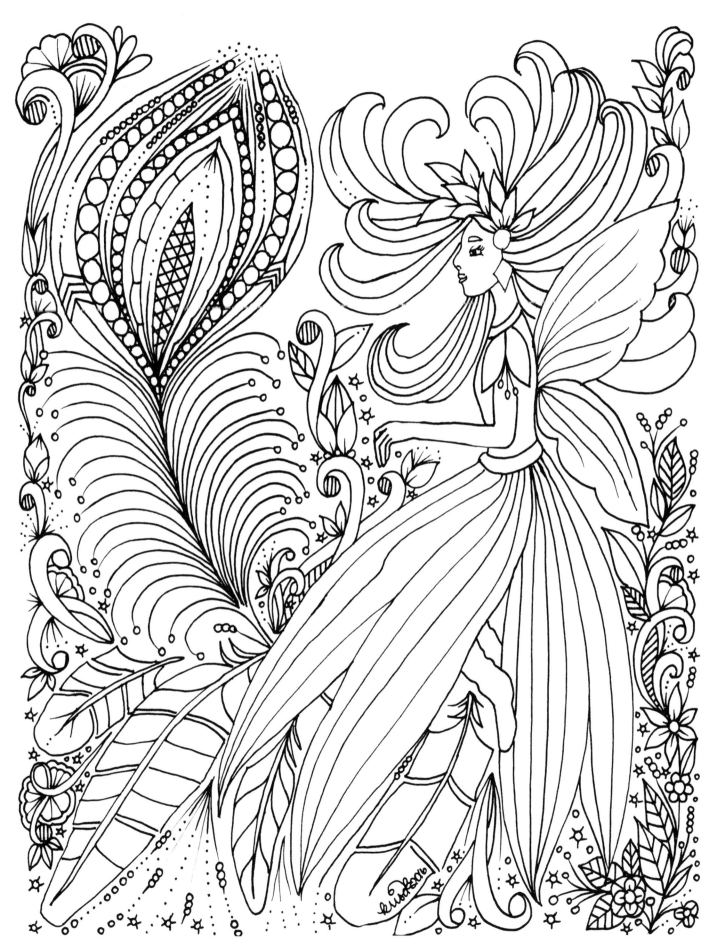

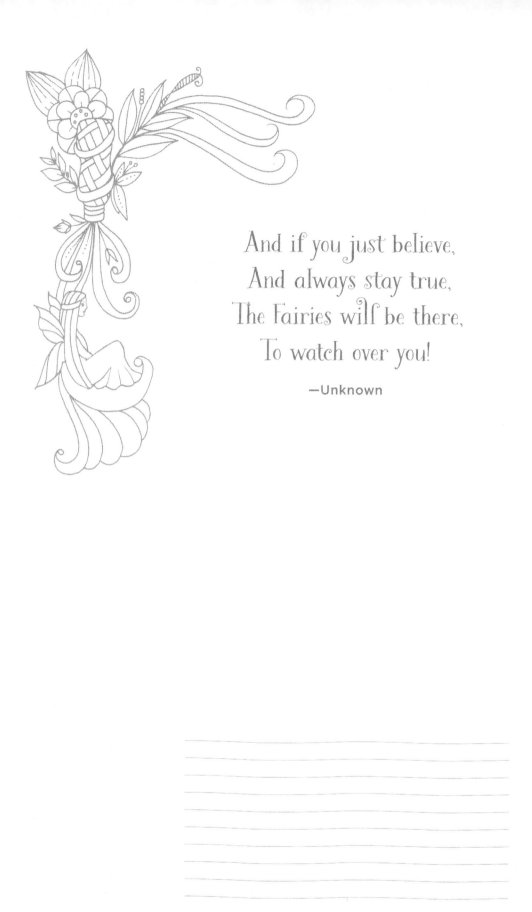

And if you just believe,
And always stay true,
The Fairies will be there,
To watch over you!

—Unknown

_____
_____
_____
_____
_____
_____
_____
_____
_____
_____

**The Fairy's Feather**

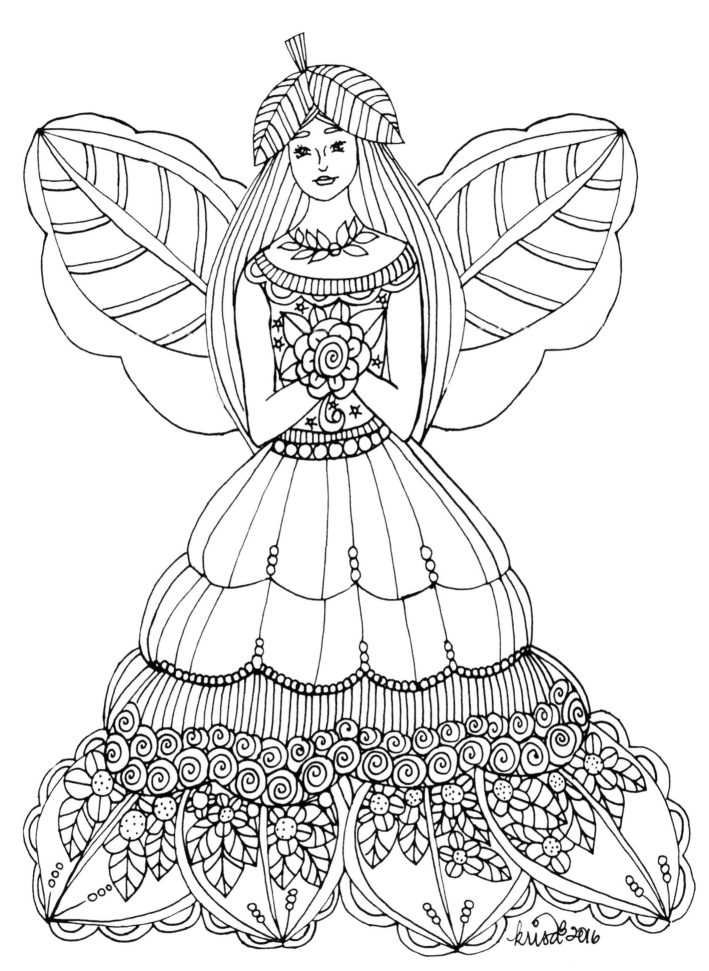

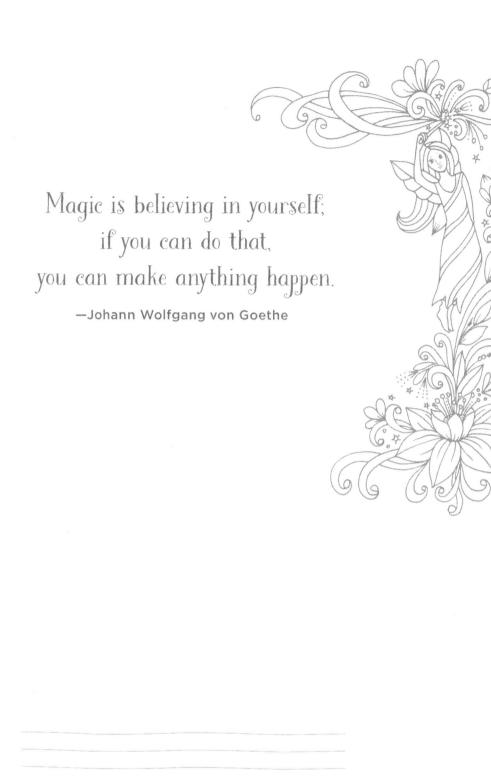

Magic is believing in yourself;
if you can do that,
you can make anything happen.

—Johann Wolfgang von Goethe

_____
_____
_____
_____
_____
_____
_____
_____
_____

**Fairy Bride**

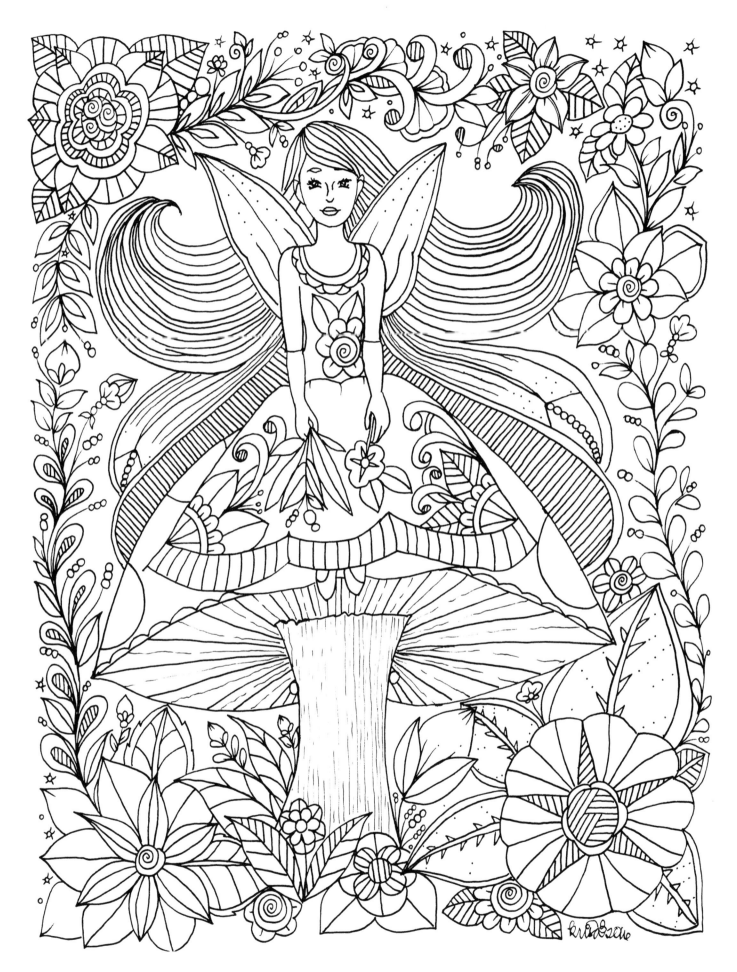

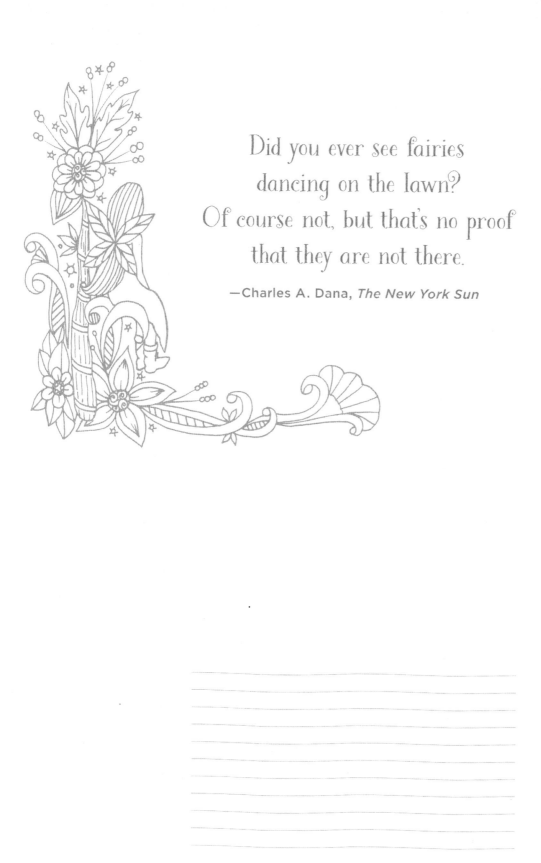

Did you ever see fairies
dancing on the lawn?
Of course not, but that's no proof
that they are not there.

—Charles A. Dana, *The New York Sun*

_____

_____

_____

_____

_____

_____

_____

_____

_____

_____

**Perched on a Mushroom**

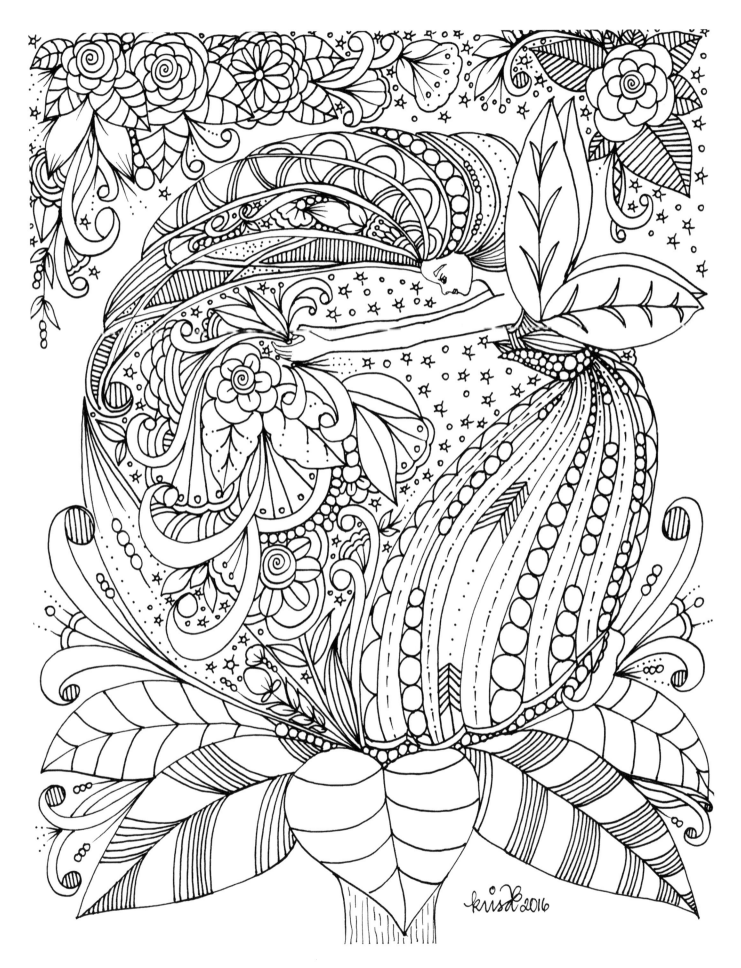

Any man can lose his hat
in a fairy-wind.

—Irish saying

_____
_____
_____
_____
_____
_____
_____
_____
_____

Magical Orb

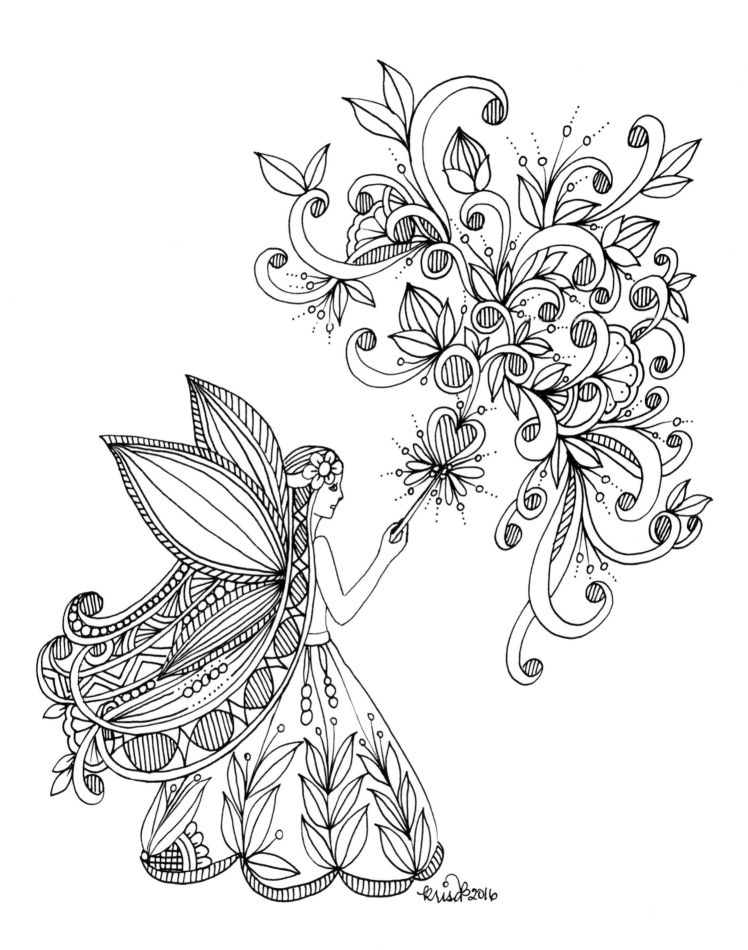

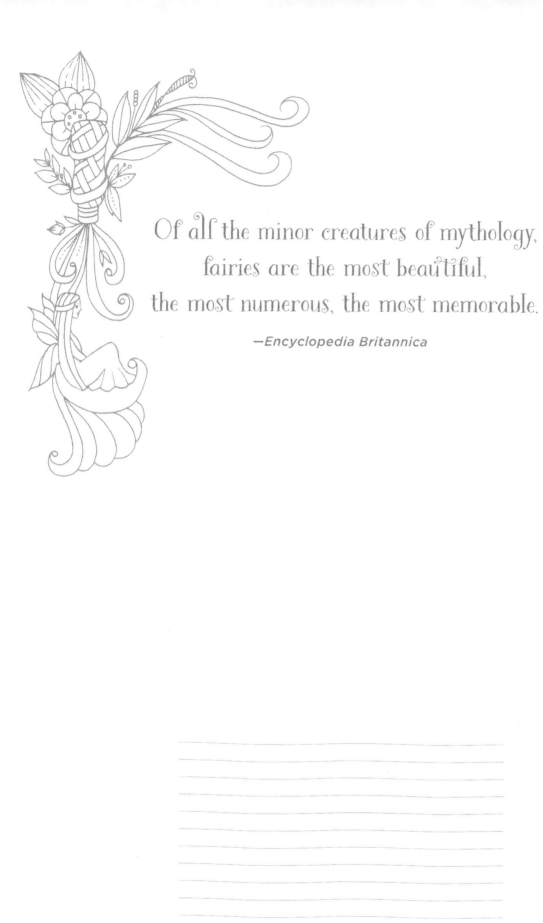

Of all the minor creatures of mythology,
fairies are the most beautiful,
the most numerous, the most memorable.

—*Encyclopedia Britannica*

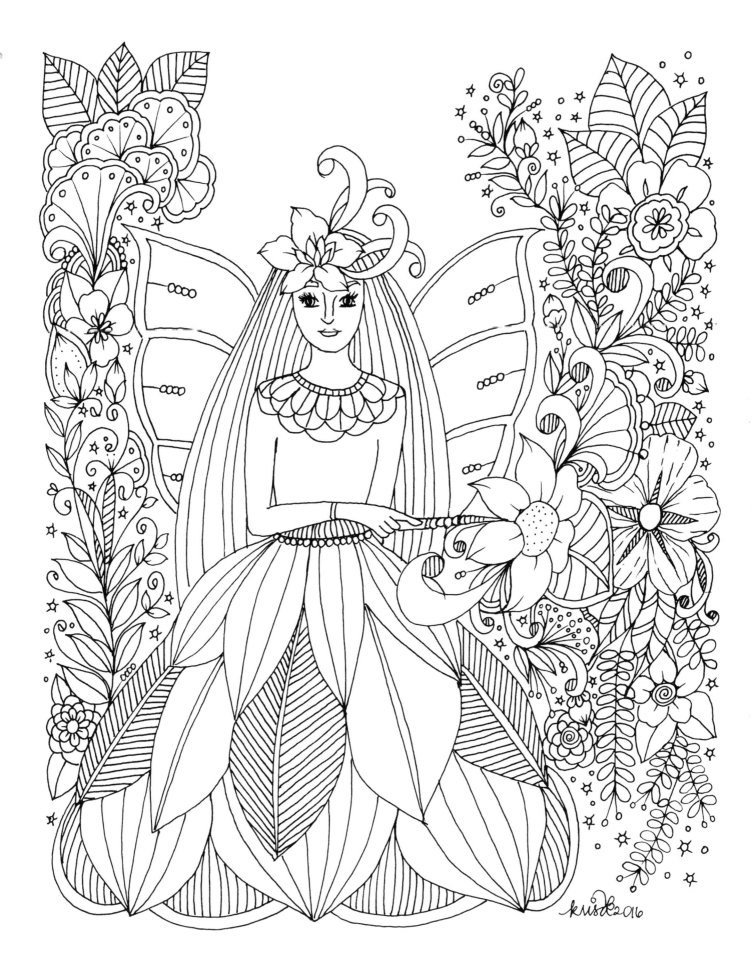

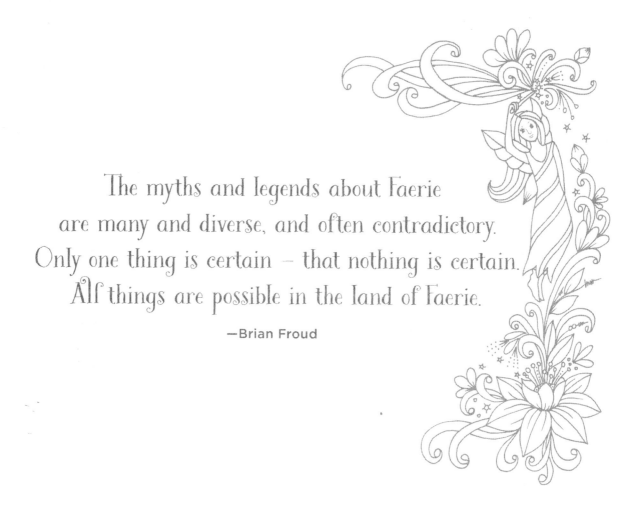

The myths and legends about Faerie
are many and diverse, and often contradictory.
Only one thing is certain – that nothing is certain.
All things are possible in the land of Faerie.

—Brian Froud

**The Fairy Princess**

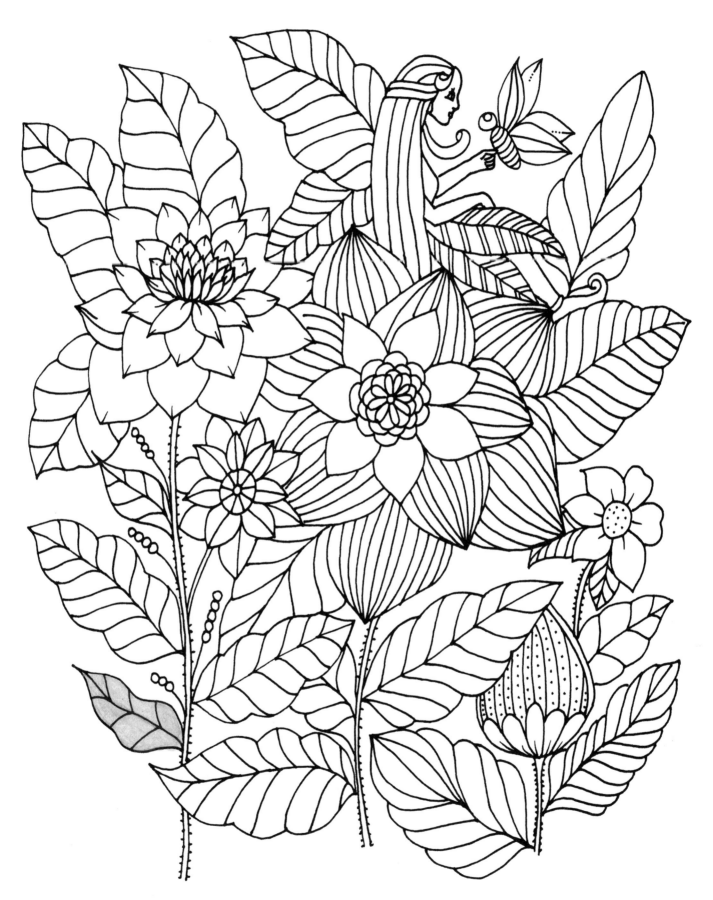

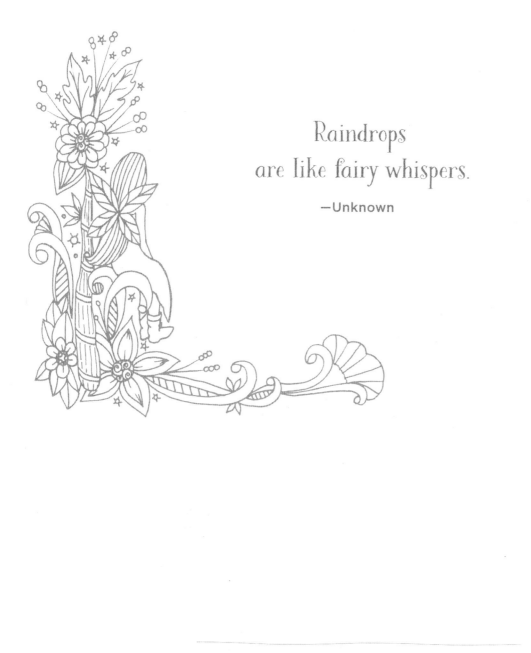

Raindrops
are like fairy whispers.

—Unknown